INDIAN BIRDS

INDIAN BIRDS

BEING A KEY TO THE COMMON BIRDS OF THE PLAINS OF INDIA

DOUGLAS DEWAR

GYAN

Published by

Gyan Publishing House
5, Ansari Road
Daryaganj, New Delhi-110002
Phone: 011-47034999, 9811692060
E-mail: books@gyanbooks.com

Distribution Network
gyanbooks.com
India, USA, Canada, UK, Australia

ISBN: 978-93-7447-000-8 (HB)

First Published, 1910

2nd Impression 2026

Printed at: Gyan Press, Delhi.

INDIAN BIRDS
Author: DOUGLAS DEWAR

INDIAN BIRDS

INDIAN BIRDS

BEING A KEY TO THE COMMON BIRDS OF THE PLAINS OF INDIA

BY DOUGLAS DEWAR

A COMPANION VOLUME TO THE BIRD VOLUMES OF "THE FAUNA OF BRITISH INDIA" & JERDON'S "BIRDS OF INDIA"

LONDON : JOHN LANE THE BODLEY HEAD
NEW YORK : JOHN LANE COMPANY MCMX

PREFACE

I FEAR that the patience of those who have been awaiting this little book must be wellnigh exhausted, so long has it been in appearing. I began it two years ago, but had to put it aside during the last few months spent in India prior to taking furlough, on account of the heavy work the threatening famine entailed; and when one is on furlough one only works at the rare times when there is nothing better to do!

The object of this book is to enable people interested in our Indian birds to identify at sight those they are likely to meet with in their compounds and during their excursions into the jungle.

There are several good systematic works on Indian ornithology, but the descriptions in these presuppose that the reader has the specimen in his hand and is able to examine it leisurely, feather by feather. To do this it is necessary to kill the bird in question

—a procedure which causes pain to many and gives pleasure to very few. Moreover, unless the seeker after knowledge has some notion as to the order to which the bird he has shot belongs, he will find that seeking it out in the four bird volumes of the *Fauna of British India* series is a task almost as hopeless as that of looking for the proverbial needle in a haystack.

Eha's truly admirable book, entitled *The Common Birds of Bombay*, gives the reader a vivid description of our common Indian birds as they appear to the field naturalist; and I heartily commend this little masterpiece to every Anglo-Indian. But even this does not enable the observer to identify in a few seconds any bird he sees, for it is not written in the form of a key. The present book is an attempt at a key to the everyday birds of the plains of India, a dictionary of birds so arranged that the budding ornithologist is able to turn up any particular bird in a few minutes. This book is, I believe, the first of its kind that has been attempted.

The method I have adopted is to classify birds according to their habits and outward appearance. Every bird has a colour, and most birds possess some anatomical peculiarity, such as a crest, a long tail, long legs, etc. Not a few have some easily recognisable habit, such as a peculiar call or manner of flight. Thus most birds will appear in at least two of my classes, and so should be easily identified by a process of elimination. When the reader thinks that he has located a bird he should turn it up in the descriptive list, which composes Part II of this book, and this will serve to confirm or correct him in his identification. Thus, to take a very easy example, the observer while out walking sees a white bird with a long tail, and a black crested head. Looking through the lists of birds under (1) those having long tails; (2) those having a crest; (3) those mainly white, he will find that the Paradise Flycatcher is the only bird that appears in all three lists. Its number in the descriptive list is (57). A perusal of entry No. 57 will confirm the diagnosis, and indicate where illustrations of the bird are to be found.

I venture to hope that this little book will enable any person to learn in a few weeks to identify nearly all the common birds of his station.

The descriptions given in Part II of the

book are short ones, and each is an attempt to depict the bird as it looks when perched in a tree or during flight. Sometimes the description given may appear to differ from those given in *The Fauna of British India*, or in Jerdon's *Birds of India*. The reason of the apparent discrepancy is that the descriptions of the birds in these latter books are those of the skins of dead birds, while mine are attempts to depict the bird as he appears in the flesh.

In a few cases I have described birds from memory, and sometimes my memory may have played me false. I shall be most grateful to anyone who will be kind enough to point out to me any errors. One of the greatest of the difficulties I have experienced is to know what birds to insert and what to leave out of this book. It is a key only to the common birds of the plains, and deals with about one-fifth of the feathered inhabitants.

I have purposely omitted the game birds from my list. These are usually shot at sight; it is therefore not necessary for me to burden this book with them. There is no lack of good books that enable the sportsman to identify the birds he has shot. I may mention Marshall and Hume's *Game Birds of India, Burmah, and Ceylon,* with its large number of coloured plates. This valuable work is out of print; but a copy is to be found in almost every Indian library. Then there is Stuart Baker's recently published *Indian Ducks and their Allies,* which contains excellent coloured plates of all Indian ducks. Those who cannot afford to purchase this sumptuous work have in Finn's *How to know the Indian Ducks,* a safe and inexpensive guide. The same author's *How to know the Indian Waders,* enables the tyro to identify any dead wader. Lastly, there is Le Mesurier's *Game, Shore, and Water Birds of India;* but this, I fear, will be found rather technical for most people. I think I have stated sufficiently clearly my reasons for excluding the majority of game birds from the present work. It now remains for me to justify the other omissions.

In order to render it comparatively easy to identify any given bird, it is necessary that the various classes shall not be too large, and the only way of securing this desideratum is to exclude all the birds that are not frequently met with.

Some may think that I have omitted certain

species that should have been included. In anticipation of such criticism I may say that I have done my best to deal impartially with my feathered friends. I have served in three provinces, viz. the United Provinces, Madras, and the Punjab, and have spent a little time on the Bombay side, and have been largely guided by my experience. It is, I admit, quite likely that some of the birds I have omitted may be very common in certain localities. I shall be glad to hear of any such with a view to adding them to a second edition should that be called for.

I would emphasise the fact that this book is a mere key, and as such is of necessity a collection of the dry bones of ornithology and devoid of any literary merit. The book will lose much of its value unless it be used in conjunction with other books, such as Jerdon's *Birds of India*, or the bird volumes of the *Fauna of British India* series, to which references are made in the case of every species mentioned. The present work is primarily a companion to either of the above volumes.

When once the common birds have been learned, it becomes comparatively easy to identify the uncommon ones and to assign to its proper family an uncommon bird.

In conclusion, let me advise every one who wishes to "learn his birds" to procure Eha's *Common Birds of Bombay*. Most of the species dealt with therein are common all over the plains.

Those who live in Calcutta will find Cunningham's *Some Indian Friends and Acquaintances*, and Finn's *Birds of Calcutta* very helpful.

Although I have, in the present work, indicated the distribution of the various birds dealt with, a local list (where it exists) will be of great assistance. The following lists have been compiled :

LOCAL LISTS OF BIRDS WHICH HAVE APPEARED IN THE JOURNAL OF THE BOMBAY NATURAL HISTORY SOCIETY

Name of Locality	Volume of Journal	No. of page
South Gujerat . . .	I	149
North Cachar	IX–XIII	—
Hylakandy District, Cachar	X–XIII	—
Gwalior	XI	136
North Canara	XI & XII	652 & 43

Preface

Name of Locality	Volume of Journal	No. of page
Andaman and Nicobar Islands	XII & XIII	—
Madhubani Subdivision of the Darbhanga District	XIII–XVI	—
Travancore	XV & XVI	—
Madras	XVI	484
Seistan	XVI	686
Chindwin, Upper Burma	XVIII	78 & 432
Bhamo District, Upper Burma	XIX	

LOCAL LISTS OF BIRDS WHICH APPEARED IN "STRAY FEATHERS"

Name of Locality	Volume of *Stray Feathers*	No. of page
Sind	I	41 & 291
Sambhur Lake . . .	I	361
Chota Nagpur	II & III	355 & 288
Upper Pegu	III	1
Mount Abu and North Gujerat	III, IV & V	437, 1, 207
Travancore	IV & VII	351 & 33
Region between Mahanadi and Godaveri rivers	V	410
Fureedpur, E. Bengal .	VII	238
South Konkan . . .	IX	1
Deccan and South Mahratta country . . .	IX	367

Name of Locality	Volume of *Stray Feathers*	No. of page
Lucknow Civil Division	IX & X	491, 1, 444
Pegu	X	175
Western Kandesh . .	X	279
Mauzeerabad, Mysore .	X	454
Belgaum	X	435
Manipur, Assam, Sylhet and Cachar . .	X	—

LOCAL LISTS OF BIRDS WHICH HAVE APPEARED IN "THE IBIS"

Name of Locality	Year of *Ibis*	No. of page
Oudh and Kumaun . .	1861	217
Kattiawar	1873	397
Dacca	1882	84
Central India . . .	1885	52
Bhamo, Upper Burma .	1888	70
Calcutta District . .	1894	39
Lucknow	1902 & 1903	470
Southern Shan States .	1901 & 1903	525
Kohat and Kurram . .	1909	90

LOCAL LISTS OF BIRDS WHICH HAVE APPEARED IN THE JOURNAL OF THE ASIATIC SOCIETY, BENGAL

Name of Locality	Volume	No. of page
Manipur	LVIII, Part II	235
Southern Shan States .	LXIX, Part II	102

CONTENTS

Contents

PART I

A. Hindustani Names of Common Birds

B. Classification according to Structural Peculiarities

C. Classification according to Colour

D. Classification according to Habits

A. HINDUSTANI NAMES OF COMMON BIRDS

Ababil, Swallow, Martin, Swift (80–90, 124 and 125).*

Ablak Maina, Pied Myna (54).

Baglā, Paddy bird (224).

Bara Kowā, Corby (1).

Batér, Quail (171).

Bāya, Baya or Weaver bird (70).

Bāz, Eagle (146); also Goshawk.

Bhairi, Peregrine Falcon.

Bhīmrāj, Racket-tailed Drongo (27).

Brāhmini Chīl, Brahminy Kite (151).

Buchanga, King Crow (25).

Būlbūl, Bulbul (15–21).

Chahā, Snipe.

Chakwá, Brahminy Duck (229).

Chandūl, Lark (97–103).

Chīl, Kite (152).

Chotā Chahā, Jack Snipe.

* In all cases the number in brackets which follows the name of a bird is the number of the bird in the Descriptive List that composes Part II of this book.

Daryā Mainā, Bank Myna (53).
Dayāl, Magpie Robin (68).
Desi Shāma, Brown Rock-chat (64).
Dhobin, Wagtail (91–94).
Fakhtā, Dove (166–169).
Gīdh, Vulture (141–145).
Golābi Mainā, Rose-coloured Starling (48).
Gonriya, Sparrow (82).
Gūgū, Dove (166–169).
Hāns, Barred-headed Goose (228).
Harre Lāl, Green Munia (78).
Harriāl, Green Pigeon (163 and 164).
Kabūtār, Pigeon (165).
Kālā Pidhā, Pied Bush Chat (61 and 62).
Kālā Tītar, Black Partridge (172).
Kārkarra, Demoiselle Crane (179).
Koil, Koel (130).
Kotwāl, King Crow (25).
Kowā, House Crow (3).
Kūlang, Common Crane (177).
Laggar, Lugger Falcon (160).
Lahtora, Shrike (34–37).
Lāl, } Amadavat (77).
Lāl Mūnia, }
Machlimār, Osprey (140).
Mainā, Myna (52).
Mohok, Crow-pheasant (131).

Mōr, Peafowl (170).
Nīlkant, Roller (115).
Pahāri Mainā, Grackle (46 and 47).
Pan-kowa, Cormorant (209–211).
Phutki, Tailor-bird, warbler (28–33).
Pīlak, Oriole (44 and 45).
Popīyā, Brain-fever bird (128).
Rāj Hans, Grey-lag Goose (227).
Safēd Gīdh, Scavenger Vulture (144 and 145).
Sārās, Sarus Crane (178).
Sāth Bhai, Seven Sisters (7–9).
Shāh Būlbūl, Paradise Flycatcher (57).
Shikrā, Shikra (158).
Siphāhi Bulbul, Red-whiskered Bulbul (20 and 21).
Sūrkiā Baglā, Cattle Egret (223).
Thampāl, King Crow (25).
Tilyer, Rose-coloured Starling (48).
Tīsa, White-eyed Buzzard (147).
Tītar, Grey Partridge (173).
Tītiri, Plover, Lapwing (183 and 184).
Tōtā, Paroquet (132–134).
Turamti, Red-headed Merlin (161).
Tūti, Rose Finch (80).
Ūllū, Owl (135–139).
Wāk, Night Heron (225).
Wokāb, Tawny Eagle (146).

B. CLASSIFICATION ACCORDING TO STRUCTURAL PECULIARITIES

I. Bill.
II. Crest.
III. Legs.
IV. Tail.
V. Sexual Dimorphism.

I. BILLS

Birds with Long Bills

1. The Sunbirds (106–108). (Very small birds with long curved bills.)

2. The Kingfishers (118–120). (Fairly long and straight.)

3. The Hornbills (121 and 122). (Big birds with long tails.)

4. The Hoopoe (123). (Bill very long and slightly curved.)

5. The Black-winged Stilt (187). (Fairly long, very slender.)

6. The Avocet (188). (Fairly long, slender, with an *upward* curve.)

7. The Curlew (189). (Very long and curved.)
8. The Whimbrel (190). (Long and curved.)
9. The Black-tailed Godwit (191).
10. The Snipes.
11. The Pelicans (207 and 208).
12. The Ibises (212–214). (Very long and slightly curved.)
13. The Spoonbill (215). (Long, straight, and flattened with a ladle-like tip.)
14. The Storks (216–221).
15. The Herons (222–225). (Fairly long and dagger-shaped.)

II. CREST

Crested birds

1. The Madras Red-vented Bulbul (15).
2. The Burmese Red-vented Bulbul (16).
3. The Bengal Red-vented Bulbul (17).
4. The Punjab Red-vented Bulbul (18).
5. The White-eared Bulbul (19).
6. The Bengal Red-whiskered Bulbul (20).
7. The Southern Red-whiskered Bulbul (21).
8. The Large Racket-tailed Drongo (27).

9. The Rose-coloured Starling (48).
10. The Brahminy Myna (51).
11. The Paradise Flycatcher (57).
12. The Crested Lark (101).
13. Sykes's Crested Lark (102).
14. The Malabar Crested Lark (103).
15. The Yellow-fronted Woodpecker (110).
16. The Golden Woodpecker (111).
17. The Pied Kingfisher (small crest) (118).
18. The Indian Hoopoe (123).
19. The Pied-crested Cuckoo (129).
20. The Common Peafowl (170).
21. The Large Cormorant (small crest) (209).

III. LEGS

Birds with very long legs

1 The White-breasted Water-hen (174). (Moderately long.)
2. The Purple Coot (175).
3. The Cranes (177–179).
4. The Stone Curlew (180).
5. The Lapwings (183 and 184).
6. The Black-winged Stilt (187).
7. The Avocet (188).

8. The Curlew (189).
9. The Whimbrel (190).
10. The Spoonbill (215).
11. The Storks (216–221).
12. The Common Flamingo (226).

Birds with legs feathered to the toe

1. The Owls (135–139).
2. The True Eagles (146).
3. The Sandgrouse.

IV. TAIL

1. *Birds with the tail deeply forked*

1. The Drongos (25–27).
2. The Swallows (88–90).
3. The Palm Swift (125).
4. The Common Kite (152). (Tail slightly forked. This distinguishes the Kite from all other raptorial birds which have round, square, or wedge-shaped tails.)
5. The Terns (200–206).

2. *Birds with long tails* (i.e. *long in proportion to rest of body*)

1. The Indian Tree-pie (5).
2. The King Crow (25).

3. The White-bellied Drongo (26).

4. The Larger Racket-tailed Drongo (27).

5. The Tailor Bird (cock in breeding plumage when the two middle feathers are prolonged as two bristles) (28).

6. The Paradise Flycatcher (cock only) (57).

7. The Shama (69).

8. The Wire-tailed Swallow (two of the tail feathers are prolonged beyond the others and look like wires. These frequently get broken off) (89).

9. The Common Indian Bee-eater (the two median tail feathers are prolonged as bristles) (116).

10. The Blue-tailed Bee-eater (the two median tail feathers are prolonged as bristles) (117).

11. The Hornbills (121 and 122).

12. The Cuckoos (128–130).

13. The Crow-pheasant (131).

14. The Large Indian Paroquet (132).

15. The Rose-ringed Paroquet (133).

16. The Western Blossom-headed Paroquet (134).

17. The Peacock (170). In this species it is not the tail, but the upper tail coverts which are elongated.

18. The Pheasant-tailed Jaçana (in breeding plumage) (182).
19. Terns (202–204).

3. Birds with a very short tail

1. The Nuthatches (23 and 24).
2. The Munias (74–79). (Fairly short.)
3. The Ashy-crowned Finch-Lark (105).
4. The Indian Pitta (109).
5. The Woodpeckers (110 and 111). (Fairly short.)
6. The Barbets (113 and 114).
7. The Kingfishers (118–120).
8. The Common Indian Swift (124).
9. The Spotted Owlet (135).
10. The Scops Owl (138).
11. The Vultures (140–142). (Fairly short.)
12. The Common Quail (171).
13. The Partridges (172 and 173).
14. The White-breasted Water-hen (174).
15. The Purple Coot (175).
16. The Coot (176).
17. The Plovers (185 and 186).
18. The Avocet (188).
19. The Black-tailed Godwit (191).
20. The Sandpipers (192–194).
21. The Little Stint (195).

22. The Pelicans (207 and 208).
23. The Cormorants (209–211).
24. The Ibises (212–214).
25. The Spoonbill (215).
26. The Egrets (223).
27. The Paddy Bird (224).
28. The Night Heron (225).
29. The Common Flamingo (226).
30. The Geese (227 and 228).
31. The Ducks (229 and 230).
32. The Little Grebe (231). (No tail at all.)

4. *Birds in which a part of the tail feathers are prolonged beyond the rest as bristles*

(*a*) *Median pair prolonged*

1. (Cock) Tailor Bird (in hot weather).
2. The Bee-eaters (116 and 117).

(*b*) *Outer pair prolonged.*

1. The Larger Racket-tailed Drongo (27). (The web reappears at the tip, so as to form a disc at the terminal part of the feather.)
2. The Wire-tailed Swallow.

V. SEXUAL DIMORPHISM

Birds in which the sexes differ greatly in appearance

1. The Common Iora (13).
2. The Minivets (39–41).
3. The Black-headed Cuckoo-Shrike (42).
4. The Orioles (44 and 45).
5. The Rose-coloured Starling (48).
6. The Indian Paradise Flycatcher (57).
7. The Pied Bush Chats (61 and 62).
8. The Indian Bush Chat (63).
9. The Indian Redstart (65).
10. The Indian Robins (66 and 67).
11. The Magpie Robin (68).
12. The Shama (69).
13. The Weaver Birds (70–73). (In breeding season only.)
14. The Indian Red Munia (79). (Particularly in breeding season.)
15. The Common Rose-Finch (180).
16. The Common Sparrow (82).
17. The Buntings (84 and 85).
18. The Ashy-crowned Finch-Lark (105).
19. The Sunbirds (106–108).
20. The Koel (130).

21. The Blossom-headed Paroquet (134).
22. The Harriers (153–157).
23. The Red Turtle Dove (169).
24. The Common Peafowl (170).
25. The Black Partridge (172).
26. The Shoveller (230). (In breeding plumage.)

C. CLASSIFICATION ACCORDING TO COLOUR

I. Black.
II. Blue.
III. Brown.
IV. Coffee or fawn colour.
V. Green.
VI. Grey.
VII. Pink.
VIII. Red.
IX. White.
X. Yellow.

Colour affords the easiest means of identifying the great majority of birds, but in many cases the colours displayed, although conspicuous and easily recognised, are not of a nature to admit of strict classification. Take, for example, the blues—various species display almost every known shade from slaty grey to turquoise, from purple to ultramarine and indigo. To attempt to distinguish in the lists between the many shades of blue would have led to inevitable confusion. I have, therefore, divided my blues into bright blue, dark blue, and slaty blue. My method is probably inartistic, but it will, I hope, facilitate the task of identification.

Again, it is no easy matter to draw the line between greyish and brownish birds, hence I have included some species under both heads. The reader should bear in mind that, while nothing is easier than to identify some birds by their colour, in the case of others colour is at the best a rough guide—one, but only one, of the clues which have to be followed up before the identity of the species can be established. In the case of Raptorial birds colour is of very little assistance, since the great majority of them are of the same colour, moreover, individuals vary greatly in colouration at different stages of their existence.

I. BLACK

1. *Birds with a quantity of black in their plumage*

(*a*) *All Black*

1. The Indian Corby (1).
2. The Raven (2).

3. The King Crow (25).

4. The Large Racket-tailed Drongo (27).

5. (Cock) Sunbirds (106 and 107). (These are really dark purple, but sometimes look black from a distance.)

6. (Cock) Koel (bill green, eyes red) (130).

7. (Young) Scavenger Vultures (144 and 145).

8. Coot (176). (White bill and shield on forehead.)

9. The Indian Shag (210).

(*b*) *Mainly Black*

1. The Indian House Crow (3).

2. The Burmese House Crow (4).

These have grey necks, darker in the latter.

3. The Malabar Whistling Thrush (11). (Patches of cobalt-blue.)

4. The Grackles (46 and 47). (Yellow wattles and white bar in wing.)

5. The Indian Starling (49). (With small yellow or whitish spots.)

6. The Common Indian Swift (124). (Smoky brown, with white bar across rump.)

7. The Palm Swift (125). (Brownish black.)

8. The Crow-Pheasant (131). (Wings chestnut brown.)

9. The Black Vulture (141). (Red head, white breast and patch on each thigh.)

10. The White-backed Vulture (143). (Very dark grey, with white back.)

11. (Cock) Black Partridge (172). (With narrow white bars and broad chestnut collar.)

12. White-breasted Water-hen (174). (Very dark grey, with white face, throat, and chest, and red under tail.)

13. The Large and Little Cormorants (209 and 211). (White throat.)

14. Black Ibis (213). (Top of head red, white patch on wing.)

2. *Black-headed birds*

1. The Indian Tree-Pie (5).
2. (Cock) Iora (13).
3. The Red-vented Bulbuls (15–19). (Small crest.)
4. The Red-whiskered Bulbuls (20 and 21). (Large pointed crest.)
5. The Minivets (39 and 40).
6. The Black-headed Cuckoo-Shrike (42).
7. The Black-headed Oriole (45).
8. The Rose-coloured Starling (48).

9. The Black-headed Myna (51).

10. The Common Myna (52). (With yellow patch of skin behind eye.)

11. The Paradise Flycatcher (57).

12. The Indian Redstart (cock in spring) (65).

13. The Magpie Robin (cock) (68).

14. The Shama (69).

15. The Black-headed Munia (74).

16. The Chestnut-bellied Munia (75).

17. The Black-headed Bunting (in spring) (84).

18. The Purple-rumped Sunbird (108). (The head and breast are not black in this species, but look black from a distance.)

19. The Crow-Pheasant (131).

20. (Male) Pied Harrier (156).

21. The Bronze-winged Jaçana (181).

22. The Red-wattled Lapwing (183). (Red wattle and sides of neck white.)

23. The Yellow-wattled Lapwing (184). (Yellow wattle, back of neck white.)

24. The Terns (especially in summer) (200–205).

25. The White Ibis (212).

26. The White-necked Stork (217). (Neck white.)

27. The Black-necked Stork (218).
28. The Night Heron (225).

3. *Black collaret or gorget or band across the breast*

1. The Bengal Red-whiskered Bulbul (20).
2. The Southern Red-whiskered Bulbul (21). (Collaret interrupted.)
3. The White Wagtail (patch on breast) (91).
4. The Ashy-crowned Finch-Lark (105). (Black cross on throat.)
5. The Common Indian Bee-eater (116).
6. Some of the Bustards. (Not dealt with in this book.)
7. The Pheasant-tailed Jaçana (182).
8. The Little Ringed Plover (186).
9. The Painted Stork (220).

4. *Black streak through the eye* (i.e. *from beak to back of head*)

1. The Chestnut-bellied Nuthatch (23).
2. The Velvet-fronted Nuthatch (24).
3. The Shrikes (34–37).
4. The Indian Oriole (44). (Rather a patch than a streak.)

5. The Ashy-crowned Finch-Lark (105).
6. The Indian Pitta (109).
7. The Bee-eaters (116 and 117).

5. *Black and another colour*

(*a*) *Black and blue*

1. The Malabar Whistling Thrush (11).
2. The Velvet-fronted Nuthatch (24). (Whitish throat, lower parts greyish.)
3. The Indian Blue Rock Pigeon (165). (Slaty blue, with black wing bars and red legs.)

(*b*) *Black and brown (chestnut)*

1. The Indian Tree-Pie (5). (Silver-grey on wings, grey bars on tail, which is long.)
2. The Common Myna (52). (White in wings and tail, yellow legs, and patch of skin behind eye.)
3. (Hen and young) Indian Paradise Fly-catcher (57).
4. (Cock) Brown-backed Indian Robin (66). (Red patch under tail.)
5. The Chestnut-bellied Munia (75).
6. The Crow-Pheasant (131). (A black bird with brown wings).

(c) Black and coffee or fawn colour

The Rose-coloured Starling (48).

(d) Black and grey

1. The Indian House Crow (3).
2. The Burmese House Crow (4).
3. The Black-headed Cuckoo-Shrike (42). (Lower abdomen white and white tip to tail.)
4. The Large Cuckoo-Shrike (43).
5. The Bank Myna (53). (Red patch of skin on side of head and buff wing bar.)

(e) Black and pink

The Rose-coloured Starling (cock) (48).

(f) Black and red

1. The Indian Scarlet Minivet (cock) (41).
2. The Short-billed Minivet (cock) (42).
3. The Indian Redstart (cock in spring) (65). (Red is dull; outer tail feathers brown.)
4. The Black-backed Indian Robin (cock) (67). (A black bird with red patch under tail.)
5. The Common Swallow (88). (Upper plumage has bluish tinge; some white in tail.)
6. The Red-rumped Swallow (90). (Upper plumage has bluish tinge.)

7. The Black Vulture (141). (White breast and patch on thigh.)

8. The Black Ibis (213). (Small white patch on wing.)

(*g*) *Black and white*

1. The White-bellied Drongo (26).
2. The Grackles (46 and 47). (Black birds with white wing bar, yellow wattles, bills, and legs.)
3. The Pied Myna (54). (Orange bill and patch behind eye.)
4. (Cock) Paradise Flycatcher (57). (White bird with long tail and black head and crest.)
5. The Fantail Flycatchers (58–60).
6. (Cock) Pied Bush Chats (61 and 62).
7. The Magpie Robin (68).
8. The Large Pied Wagtail (92).
9. The Indian Pied Kingfisher (118). (Spotted black and white like a Hamburgh fowl.)
10. The Common Indian Swift (124). (Very dark brown, with white bar across back.)
11. The Pied-crested Cuckoo (129).
12. The Indian White-backed Vulture (143). (Very dark grey, with white back.)
13. (Cock) Pied Harrier (155).
14. The Coot (176).

15. (Cock) Black-winged Stilt (187). (Long-legged white bird with black back and wings.)

16. The Avocet (188). (White wading bird with black markings.)

17. The Indian Skimmer (206). (Dark brown and white.)

18. The Cormorants (209 and 211). (Black birds with white throat.)

19. The White Ibis (212). (White bird with black head.)

20. The White Stork (216). (White bird with black in wings; red bill and legs.)

21. The White-necked Stork (217). (Black bird with white neck and lower parts.)

22. The Black-necked Stork (218).

23. The Painted Stork (220).

24. The Open-bill (221).

(*b*) *Black and yellow*

1. (Cock) Iora (in summer) (13). (Two white bars in wing.)

2. (Hen) Scarlet and Short-billed Minivets (39 and 40).

3. The Orioles (44 and 45).

4. The Grackles (46 and 47). (Black birds with yellow bill, wattles, and legs, and white wing bar.)

6. *Black and two other colours*

(*a*) *Black, blue, and white*

The Velvet-fronted Blue Nuthatch (24). (The white is greyish.)

(*b*) *Black, brown, and white*

1. The Black-tailed Godwit (191).
2. The Barred-headed Goose (228). (Plumage greyish brown; bill and legs yellow.)

(*c*) *Black, chestnut, and white*

1. (Cock) Indian Bush Chat (63).
2. The Shama (69).
3. The Black-headed Munia (74).
4. The Chestnut-bellied Munia (75).
5. (Cock) Black Partridge (172).
6. The Bronze-winged Jaçana (181).

(*d*) *Black, fawn-colour, and white*

The Indian Hoopoe (123).

(*e*) *Black, grey, and white*

1. The Indian Grey Shrike (34).
2. The Black-headed Cuckoo-Shrike (42).
3. The White Wagtail (91).
4. The Ashy-crowned Finch-Lark (105).

5. The Gulls (196–199) }
6. The Terns (200–205) } Wings very pale grey
7. The Night Heron (225).
8. The Barred-headed Goose (228). (Greyish brown; bill and legs yellow.)

(*f*) *Black, pink, and white*

The Common Flamingo (226).

II. BLUE

Birds with blue in their plumage

(*a*) *Bright blue*

1. The Common Green Bulbul (14). (Bright green bird with blue moustache.)
2. The Indian Pitta (109).
3. The Indian Roller or "Blue Jay" (115). (Wings and tail composed of light and dark blue bars.)
4. The Common Indian Bee-eater (116). (A green bird with turquoise throat, black streak through eye, and two long bristle-like feathers in tail.)
5. The Blue-tailed Bee-eater (117).
6. The Common Kingfisher (119).
7. The White-breasted Kingfisher (120).

8. The Green Parrots (132–134). (Green birds with blue in their long tails.)

9. The Common Peafowl (170).

10. The Purple Coot (175). (A large purple-blue bird with red bill, legs, and frontal shield.)

(*b*) *Dark blue*

1. The Malabar Whistling Thrush (11). (A black bird with cobalt patches.)

2. The Nuthatches (23 and 24). (Little short-tailed birds which go about in small flocks and pick insects off the bark of trees.)

3. The Swallows (88–90). (Upper parts glossy, dark blue.)

4. The Indian Roller or "Blue Jay" (115). (Wings and tail composed of light and dark blue bars.)

(*c*) *Slaty or greyish blue*

The Indian Blue Rock Pigeon (165).

(*d*) *Blue and black birds*

(*Vide* Black and blue birds.)

III. BROWN

The number of birds of which the predominating hue is brownish is very considerable, and as these usually have nothing striking about their appearance, they are among the most difficult birds to identify. Birds which appear to be a uniform earthy brown will be found on closer inspection almost invariably to be brighter in hue below than above. This is largely counteracted by the fact that the lower parts are in the shade. Most birds which look a uniform earthy brown are in reality a cream colour below, and are described as such in systematic works on ornithology. But as this book is intended for the field naturalist, I shall describe them as they appear to the ordinary observer.

1. *Birds whose general hue is earthy brown*

(*a*) *Those smaller than the sparrow*

1. The Indian Tailor Bird (28). (This flits about among the leaves. The note is a loud *to-wee, to-wee, to-wee*. When the bird calls a small black band may be seen at each side of the neck. In the breeding season the two

middle tail feathers of the cock grow over an inch longer than the others and project beyond them like bristles. A very familiar wren-like bird. The brown has a greenish tint.)

2. Sykes's Tree-warbler (29). (Not unlike a solidly built wren, with a tail of average length, and not short like that of the wren.)

3. The Streaked Wren-warbler (30). (This is distinguished from other warblers by the fact that its upper plumage is streaked with dark brown.)

4. The Ashy Wren-warbler (31). (Makes a curious snapping noise as it flits about the bushes.)

5. The Indian Wren-warblers (32 and 33). (Slender and loosely-knit, and make no snapping noise.)

6. The Brown Flycatcher (55). (Characterised by its short tail and the fact that it constantly makes little sallies into the air after insects.)

7. (Hen) Indian Bush Chat (63). (Reddish brown. Cock quite differently coloured.)

8. The White-throated Munia (76). (Very thick bill, white throat and rump, and a note like the twitter of the sparrow; usually seen in small flocks.)

9. The Indian Sand-martin (86). (Swallow-like flight; nests in sandbanks.)

10. The Dusky Crag-martin (87). (Swallow-like flight; builds mud nest.)

11. (Hen) Sunbirds (106–108). (Pale yellow under parts, longish curved bill, sometimes hovers in the air on rapidly vibrating wings. Cocks gaily coloured.)

(*b*) *The size of, or a little larger than, the sparrow*

1. The Common Babbler (6). (A brown bird with a number of dark streaks. As it runs along it carries its tail along the ground, hence its name, "The Rat Bird.")

2. The White-browed Bulbul (22). (Pale yellow patch under the tail, white eyebrow. It has a very cheery call.)

3. The Common Woodshrike (38). (Broad white eyebrow, outer tail feathers white; a pretty mellow note—*tanti tuia.*)

4. (Hen) Pied Bush Chat (61 and 62). (Reddish brown, with black tail; cock more strikingly coloured.)

5. The Brown Rock Chat (64). (Robin-like in habits; continually bobs its head.)

6. (Hen) Indian Robins (67 and 68). (Brick-red patch under tail. Tail often carried erect.)

7. Weaver Birds (70–73). (Stout bill. Cock becomes showy in breeding season.)

8. (Hen) Rose Finch (80). (Two white bars in wing.)

9. Yellow-throated sparrow (81). Yellow patch on throat.)

10. (Hen) Common Sparrow (82).

11. The Grey-necked Bunting (83). Thickish bill, some dark streaks in plumage and white in tail).

12. (Hen) Black-headed Bunting (84). (Dull yellow under parts and bright yellow patch under the tail.)

13. The Pipits (95 and 96). (Longish legs; dark streaks in plumage. Feed on ground, but take refuge in trees when disturbed.)

14. The Larks (97 and 98). (Feed on ground; never perch in trees; some soar in the air and sing.)

15. The Bush Larks (99 and 100). (Distinguished from the true larks in perching in bushes when they sometimes take short flights into the air. Distinguished from the pipits in having no white in the tail.)

16. The Crested Larks (101–103). (Feed

on ground ; sing in air ; never perch in bushes. Crested heads ; no white in tail.)

17. The Common Wryneck (112). (Woodpecker-like habits. It twists its head from side to side continually. Its plumage is much streaked, speckled, and spotted.)

18. The Spotted Owlet (135). (Plumage much spotted and barred with white. Eyes in front of head. Comes out at sunset and sets up a loud chuckling chatter. Legs feathered to the toes.)

19. The Scops Owl (138). (Differs from the Spotted Owlet in having " horns " or ear-tufts. Note a single hoot, which is repeated regularly at intervals of about ten seconds.)

20. The Jungle Owlet (139). (Distinguished from the Spotted Owlet by its call and by the fact that it is far less often seen.)

21. The Kentish Plover (185). (White collar. Found in flocks on the sea coasts.)

22. The Little Ringed Plover (186). (Like the Kentish Plover, but distinguished from it by having a black band across the white throat.)

23. The Little Stint. (Wading birds, which occur in large flocks on shallow water.)

(*c*) *About the size of a myna*

1. The Jungle Babbler (7). (An untidy-looking bird, which goes about in small flocks of half a dozen, feeding on the ground ; very noisy ; flight feeble.)

2. The White-headed Babbler (8). (As above, but the crown of the head is greyish white. Found only in S. India.)

3. The Rufous-tailed Babbler (9). (Habits like those of the two species just cited ; tail has a reddish tinge.)

4. The Common Indian Nightjar (126). (Plumage much mottled ; crepuscular in its habits ; it flits about at dusk hawking insects.)

5. Horsfield's Nightjar (127). (A large edition of above.)

6. The Common Hawk Cuckoo (128). (Plumage much barred, like that of a bird of prey. Its loud crescendo call, a reiterated " brain-fever," has made it familiar to all.)

7. The Shikra and the Sparrow-hawk (158 and 159). (Ashy grey birds with dark cross-bars to the feathers.)

8. The Common Quail (171). (A good deal smaller than a myna ; legs short ; plumage

much barred with black. Lives exclusively on the ground.)

9. The Sandpipers (192–194). (Long-legged birds with white under parts and short tails, which occur in marshes or at the water's edge.)

(*d*) *Large birds. Bigger than a crow*

1. The Common Grey Hornbill (121). (A large brownish-grey bird with long tail and big beak.)

2. The Malabar Grey Hornbill (122). (Like the above, but found chiefly on the west coast.)

3. The larger Owls (136 and 137). (Much barred and spotted. Night birds, with the eyes forwardly directed.)

4. The great majority of Birds of Prey (140–162). (Plumage usually much barred.)

5. The Grey Partridge (174). (Plumage much barred. Does not perch in trees; runs very fast; characteristic call.)

6. The Stone Curlew (180). (Black streaks in plumage, some white in wings and tail; legs and bill yellow.)

7. The Curlew (189). (A wading bird. Long curved bill.)

8. The Whimbrel (190). (A small edition of the Curlew.)

9. The Pond Heron (124). (Found at the water's edge. Flight transforms it into a milk-white bird.)

10. The Night Heron (225). (Head black. Its cry " wāāk " is heard at sunset.)

11. The Grey-lag Goose (227). (Bill and legs dirty pink.)

2. *Birds with chocolate or rich brown in plumage*

1. The Indian Treepie (5). (Long tail, silver grey on wings.)

2. The Yellow-eyed Babbler (10). (Cinnamon-brown bird with white breast.)

3. The Brown Shrike (37).

4. The Brahminy Myna (51). (Buff and grey bird with a black head.)

5. The Common Myna (52). (Yellow patch of skin at side of head.)

6. The Indian Bush Chat (63).

7. (Hen) Indian Redstart (65).

8. (Hen) Indian Robins (66 and 67). (Cock also in one species.)

9. The Munias (74, 75, and 77). (Not 76.)

10. The Red-headed Bunting (85).

11. The White-breasted Kingfisher (120).

12. The Crow-Pheasant (131). (Black bird with reddish-brown wings.)

13. The Barn Owl (136).

14. The Short-eared Owl (137).

15. The Brahminy Kite (151). (Reddish-brown bird with white head.)

16. The Kestrel (162). (Wings reddish brown.)

17. (Cock) Red Turtle Dove (168). (Wings reddish brown.)

18. The Black Partridge (172).

19. The Bronze-winged Jaçana (181). (Runs about on water weeds.)

20. The Red and Yellow-wattled Lapwings (183 and 184). (Back and wings bronzy brown.)

21. The Glossy Ibis (214).

22. The Shoveller (230).

23. The Indian Little Grebe (231).

3. *Brown and black birds.*

(*Vide* Black and brown birds.)

4. COFFEE OR FAWN COLOUR

1. *A fawn-coloured bird with black and white wings and tail*

The Indian Hoopoe (123).

2. Black and coffee colour

(Young) Rose-coloured Starling (40).

V. GREEN

Birds in the plumage of which bright green predominates

1. The Indian White-eye (12). (Greenish yellow above, bright yellow below.)
2. (Hen) Iora (13). (Lower parts yellow; two white wing bars.)
3. The Common Green Bulbul * (14).
4. The Green Munia (78). (Yellow under parts; red beak.)
5. The Indian Pitta (109). (Back and shoulders only are green.)
6. The Green Barbet * (113). (Brown patch of skin behind the eye.)
7. The Coppersmith (114). (Olive green.)
8. The Bee-eaters * (116 and 117). (Two middle tail feathers prolonged as bristles.)
9. The Paroquets * (132–134). (Long tails.)
10. The Green Pigeons (163 and 164).
11. The Bronze-winged Jaçana (181). (Wings only greenish bronze. Runs about on floating plants.)

* These are practically green all over.

12. (Cock) Shoveller Duck (230). (Head, neck, and wing patch (speculum) only glossy green.)

VI. GREY

1. *Prevailing hue grey*

N.B.—Many birds are so coloured that it is not easy to know whether to class them as grey or as brown birds.

1. The Indian Grey Shrike (34). (Broad black band through eye.)
2. The Small Minivet (41). (Upper parts slaty grey.)
3. The Cuckoo-Shrikes (42 and 43).
4. The Grey-headed Myna (50).
5. The Bank Myna (53). (Grey and black bird with red patch of skin on side of head.)
6. (Hen) Magpie Robin (68). (Grey and white bird.)
7. The Grey and Grey-headed Wagtails (93 and 94). (Upper parts bluish grey, lower yellow.)
8. The Ashy-crowned Finch-Lark (105). (Upper parts ashy grey.)
9. The Grey Hornbills (121 and 122). (Large greyish-brown birds with the tail long.)
10. The Pale, Montagu's and the Hen Harriers (153–155).

11. The Shikra (158). (Narrow rust-coloured bars on lower parts.)

12. The Sparrow-hawk (159). (Rust-coloured bars on abdomen.)

13. The Indian Blue Rock Pigeon (165). (Bluish grey with two black bars in wing.)

14. The Doves (166–169).

15. The Grey Partridge (173). (Plumage greyish brown and much barred.)

16. The Cranes (177–179). (Large French-grey birds with long shanks.)

17. The Grey Pelican (208). (Pale grey; enormous bill.)

18. The Adjutant (219).

19. The Common Heron (222).

20. The Barred-headed Goose.

2. *The head only grey*

1. The White-headed Babbler (8). (Crown of head is often greyish rather than white.)

2. The Bay- and Rufous-backed Shrikes (35 and 36). (Broad black band through eye.)

3. The Grey-headed Flycatcher (56).

4. (Cock) Indian Redstart (65). (Head and neck grey in early winter.)

5. (Cock) Black-headed Bunting (84). (In early winter. Under parts yellow.)

3. *Grey and black*

(*Vide* Black and grey.)

4. *Grey, black, and white*

(*Vide* Black, grey, and white.)

5. *Grey and red bird*

The Kestrel (162). (Head, neck, and tail grey; back and wings brick red.)

6. *Grey and white*

1. (Hen) Magpie Robin (68).
2. The Gulls (196–199). (White birds with very pale grey wings.)
3. The Terns (200–205). (White birds with very pale grey wings.)
4. The Common Heron (222). (Under parts white.)

VII. PINK

1. The Rose-coloured Starling (48). (Black and deep rose-coloured pink.)
2. The Common Flamingo (226). (Legs long and deep pink; wings white, black, and cerise.)

VIII. RED

1. *Birds with red in plumage, or having red wattles or red skin on head*

(*a*) *Bright red*

1. The Red-vented Bulbuls (15–18).
2. The Red-whiskered Bulbuls (20 and 21).
3. The Minivets * (39–41).
4. The Bank Myna (53).
5. The Indian Redstart * (65).
6. The Indian Robins (66 and 67).
7. The Amadavat * (79).
8. (Cock) Common Rose-Finch (80).
9. The Purple-rumped Sunbird (108). (Back dull crimson.)
10. The Pitta (109).
11. (Cock) Yellow-fronted Pied Woodpecker (110).
12. Golden-backed Woodpecker (111).
13. The Crimson-breasted Barbet (114).
14. The Green Parrots (131–133).
15. The Black Vulture (141).
16. The Purple Coot (175). (Red shield on forehead.)

* These birds are conspicuously red.

17. The Common Crane (177). (Red patch across back of head.)

18. The Sarus (178). (Red — not very bright—head and neck.)

19. The Red-wattled Lapwing (183).

20. The Black Curlew (213). (Back of head red.)

21. The Flamingo (226). (White and cerise.)

(*b*) *Dull red* (*chestnut, bay, or maroon*)

1. The Chestnut-bellied Nuthatch (23).
2. The Bay- and Rufous-backed Shrikes (35 and 36).
3. The Shama (69).
4. The Chestnut-bellied Munia (75).
5. The Red-headed Bunting (85).
6. The Swallows (88–90).
7. The Rufous-tailed Finch-Lark (104).
8. The Common Kingfisher (119).
9. The Crow-Pheasant (131).
10. The Brahminy Kite (151).
11. The Red-headed Merlin (161).
12. The Kestrel (162).
13. (Cock) Red Turtle Dove (169).
14. The White-breasted Water-hen (174).
15. The Bronze-winged Jaçana (181).

16. The Ruddy Sheldrake (229). (The red is very yellowish.)
17. The Shoveller (230).
18. The Indian Little Grebe (231).

2. *Red crest*

The Woodpeckers (110 and 111).

3. *Red-legged birds*

1. The Coppersmith (114).
2. The Common Kingfisher (119).
3. The White-breasted Kingfisher (120).
4. The Indian Blue Rock Pigeon (165).
5. The Doves (166–168).
6. The Partridges (172 and 173). (Dull brownish red.)
7. The Purple Coot (175).
8. The Sarus (178).
9. The Black-winged Stilt (187).
10. The Laughing Gull (196).
11. The Brown-headed Gull (197).
12. The Whiskered Tern (200).
13. The Indian River Tern (203).
14. The Black-bellied Tern (204). (Orange red.)
15. The Indian Skimmer (206).

16. The Black Ibis (213).
17. The Storks (216–218).
18. The Common Flamingo (226). (Deep pink.)
19. The Grey-lag Goose. (Dirty pinkish red.)
20. The Shoveller (230). (Yellowish red.)

4. *Red patch of feathers under the tail, birds with*

1. The Red-vented Bulbuls (15–18).
2. The Red-whiskered Bulbuls (20 and 21).
3. The Indian Robins (66 and 67).
4. The Indian Pitta (109).
5. The White-breasted Water-hen (174).

5. *Red patch of feathers on shoulder, birds with*

1. The Alexandrine Paroquet (131).
2. The Blossom-headed Paroquet (133).

6. *Red patch of skin on side of head, birds with*

1. The Bank Myna (53).
2. The Red-wattled Lapwing (183).

7. *Red and black*

(*Vide* Black and red.)

IX. WHITE

1. *Birds of which the plumage is pure white*

1. The Spoonbill (215).
2. The Egrets (223).

2. *Birds in the plumage of which white largely predominates*

1. (Cock) Paradise Flycatcher (57). (Black head and crest.)
2. The Black-winged Stilt (187). (Back and wings black in cock, brown in hen.)
3. The Avocet (188). (Several black markings.)
4. The Gulls (196–199).
5. The Terns (200–205).
6. The Dalmatian Pelican (207). (Some black in wings.)
7. The White Ibis (212). (Black head and neck; long curved bill.)
8. The White Stork (216). (Black in wings; red legs.)
9. The Black-necked Stork (218). (Black in wings; head, neck, and shoulders black; legs red.)

10. The Painted Stork (220). (Black wings and bar across breast; legs brown.)

11. The Open-bill (221). (Dirty white, with black on wings, shoulders, and tail.)

12. The Common Flamingo (226). (Some cerise in the plumage.)

3. *Dull-coloured bird whose wings appear all white when flying*

The Pond Heron (224).

4. *White bar in wing, birds with*

1. The Grey, Bay- and Rufous-backed Shrikes (34–36).
2. The Grackles (46 and 47).
3. The Common Myna (52).
4. The Pied Bush Chats (61 and 62).
5. (Cock) Indian Robins (66 and 67.)
6. The Magpie Robin (68).
7. The Large Pied Wagtail (92).
8. The Indian Pitta (109).
9. The White-breasted Kingfisher (120).
10. The Pied-crested Cuckoo (129).
11. The Red- and Yellow-wattled Lapwings (183 and 184).
12. The Common Sandpiper (192). (Very narrow white bar.)

5. *Two white bars in wing, birds with*

1. The Iora (13).
2. (Hen) Rose-Finch (80).

6. *White cheeks, birds with*

1. The White-eared Bulbul (19).
2. The Red-whiskered Bulbuls (20 and 21). (Also a small patch of crimson feathers on cheeks.)
3. The Chestnut-bellied Nuthatch (23).
4. The Pied Myna (54).
5. The Indian Bush Chat (63). (The patch in this species is on the sides of the neck, not on the cheeks.)
6. (Cock) Sparrow (82).
7. The Ashy-crowned Finch-Lark (105).
8. The Golden-backed Woodpecker (111). (The white on the cheeks is intersected by a number of thin black lines.)
9. The Black Partridge (172).
10. The Common Crane (177). (In this species the white runs down each side of the long neck.)
11. The Red-wattled Lapwing (183). (Here a white band runs from eye down the neck.)
12. The Yellow-wattled Lapwing (184).

(Here a white band runs from eye to eye round the back of the head.)

7. Ring of white feathers round eye

1. The Indian White-eye (12).
2. The Brown Flycatcher (55). (Ring not very conspicuous.)
3. The Grey-necked Bunting (83). (Ring not very conspicuous.)

8. White and black

(*Vide* Black and white.)

9. White, black, and blue

(*Vide* Black, blue, and white.)

10. White, black, and brown

(*Vide* Black, brown, and white.)

11. White, black, and chestnut

(*Vide* Black, chestnut, and white.)

12. White, grey, and black

(*Vide* Black, grey, and white.)

13. White, pink, and black

(*Vide* Black, pink, and white.)

X. YELLOW

1. *Birds with bright yellow in the plumage*

1. The Indian White-eye (12).

2. The Iora (13).

3. The Common Green Bulbul (14). (Patch of yellow on forehead.)

4. The White-eared Bulbul (19). (Yellow patch under the tail.)

5. The White-browed Bulbul (22). (Pale yellow patch under tail.)

6. (Hen) Minivets (39, 40, and 41).

7. The Orioles (44 and 45).

8. The Grackles or Hill Mynas (46 and 47). (Black birds with yellow beak, legs, and wattles.)

9. The Common Myna (52). (Yellow beak, legs, and patch of skin behind eye.)

10. The Pied Myna (54). (Orange patch of skin behind eye.)

11. The Grey-headed Flycatcher (56).

12. (Cock) Bayas (at breeding season) (70–73).

13. The Green Munia (78).

14. The Yellow-throated Sparrow (81).

15. The Black- and Red-headed Buntings (84 and 85).

16. The Grey and Grey-headed Wagtails (93 and 94).

17. (Cock) Purple-rumped Sunbird (108).

18. The Indian Pitta (109).

19. The Yellow-fronted Woodpecker (110). (Spotted black and white bird with yellow forehead.)

20. The Golden-backed Woodpecker (111). (Back golden yellow.)

21. The Pheasant-tailed Jaçana (182). (Back of neck golden yellow in breeding plumage.)

22. The Yellow-wattled Lapwing (184).

23. The Cattle Egret (in breeding plumage) (223). (Yellow plumes grow from back of head.)

2. *Birds with bright yellow or orange legs*

1. The Yellow-eyed Babbler (10).

2. The Grackles (46 and 47).

3. The Mynas (51–53).

4. The Common Hawk-Cuckoo (128). (Not very bright.)

5. The majority of Birds of Prey. (The yellow varies from dull to bright.)

6. The Green Pigeons (163 and 164).

7. The Black Partridge (172). (Reddish orange.)

8. The Stone Curlew (180).
9. The Red- and Yellow-wattled Lapwings (183–184).
10. The Herring-Gulls (198 and 199).
11. The Little Tern (205). (Orange in summer, brownish in winter.)
12. The Barred-headed Goose (228).
13. The Shoveller (230).

3. *Birds with dull-coloured upper plumage and bright yellow under parts*

1. The Indian White-eye (12).
2. The Iora (13).
3. The Grey-headed Flycatcher (56).
4. The Green Munia (78).
5. The Black- and Red-headed Buntings (84 and 85).
6. The Grey and Grey-headed Wagtails (93 and 94).

4. *Yellow patch of feathers under the tail, birds with*

1. The White-eared Bulbul (19).
2. The White-browed Bulbul (22).

5. *Yellow patch of feathers on the throat, bird with*

The Yellow-throated Sparrow (81).

6. *Yellow patch of skin on side of head or yellow wattles, birds with*

1. The Grackles (46 and 47).
2. The Common and Pied Mynas (52 and 54).
3. The Yellow-wattled Lapwing (184).

7. *Yellowish red*

The Brahminy Duck (229). (This bird is mainly of a ruddy yellow hue.)

8. *Yellow and black*

(*Vide* Black and yellow.)

XI. BIRDS OF MANY COLOURS

9. *Birds in the plumage of which at least four bright colours appear*

1. (Cock) Purple-rumped Sunbird (108).
2. The Indian Pitta (109).
3. The Coppersmith (114).
4. The Common Kingfisher (119).
5. The Green Pigeons (163).
6. The Peafowl (170).

D. CLASSIFICATION ACCORDING TO HABITS

I. Birds having remarkable cries.

II. Birds whose nests are likely to be found in any garden in the plains.

III. Birds that habitually sit on exposed perches.

IV. Birds that go about in flocks.

V. Flight.

VI. Feeding habits.

VII. Birds which habitually carry the tail almost vertically.

Since habits of birds vary according to circumstances, none of the lists given are exhaustive. They merely serve as rough guides. Thus, if a nest be found in the compound it is in all probability the nest of one of the species set forth in the list given, but it may, of course, belong to some other species. The list is nevertheless useful, as out of twenty nests found in any garden in the plains nineteen of them will also certainly belong to birds set forth in my list. Having determined that a given bird in all probability belongs to one of these species, it should not be difficult to arrive at its name by a process of elimination.

I. BIRDS HAVING REMARKABLE CRIES

Call	Name of Bird	No. of Bird in Part II
A loud metallic *coch-lee, coch-lee*, or *cogee, cogee*	Indian Tree-pie	5
Squeaks like that of a revolving axle that requires oiling	The Seven Sisters .	6
A striking whistle, like that of a human being	The Idle Schoolboy	11
A sweet little tinkling song .	The Bulbuls .	15–22
A cheery whistle, heard chiefly at dawn, which Cunningham describes as "chēyk, chĕchi chĕyk, chēyk chĕchi chēy chēyh"	The King Crow .	25
A loud *to-wee, to-wee, to-wee* .	The Tailor Bird . .	28
A snapping noise	Ashy Wren-warbler .	31

Classification According to Habits

Call	Name of Bird	No. of Bird in Part II
A pretty, mellow *tanti-tuia* .	The Wood-shrike .	38
A loud, mellow, *peeho, peeho* .	The Orioles .	44 & 45
Keeky, keeky, keeky . . . churr, churr, kok, kok, kok . . .	The Common Myna	52
A whistle of about six notes, like the first bars of the "Guards Valse"	The Fan-tailed Fly-catchers	58-60
A song like that of a canary .	Purple Sun-bird . .	107
A loud, screaming call . . .	Golden-backed Wood-pecker .	111
A loud, monotonous, penetrating *kutur kutur, kuturuk* .	Green Barbet . .	113
A monotonous, metallic *tonk, tonk, tonk,* like the tapping of a hammer on metal . .	The Copper-smith .	114
A loud, rattling scream . . .	White-breasted Kingfisher	120
A low *ūk, ūk, ūk*	The Hoopoe . .	123

Call	Name of Bird	No. of Bird in Part II
A shrill, trembling scream . .	The Swift	124
A sound like a stone sliding over ice	The Common Nightjar	126
Chuk, chuk, chuk, like the tapping of a plank with a hammer	Horsfield's Nightjar	127
A *crescendo* "brain-fever, *brain-fever,* BRAIN-FEVER" . . .	Brain-fever Bird . .	128
A *crescendo* "ku-il, *ku-il,* KU-IL"	The Koel	130
A low, sonorous, owl-like *whoot, whoot, whoot*	The Crow-Pheasant	131
Loud screams uttered during flight	The Paroquets	132–134
"A torrent of squeak and chatter and gibberish," *kucha, kwachee, kwachee, kwachee, khwachee* rapidly uttered in a shrieking, chattering tone	The Spotted Owlet .	135
A weird screech, heard at night	The Barn Owl . .	136
A single hoot repeated monotonously at regular intervals of ten seconds, *oomp* . . .	The Scops Owl . .	138

Classification According to Habits

Call	Name of Bird	No. of Bird in Part II
At early dawn. "*Turtuck, turtuck, turtuck, turtuck, turtuck, turtuck, tuckatu, chatucka tuckatuck.* The words or dissyllables sounding rather low at first and with considerable pauses between, and the intervals decreasing and the tone getting louder till they end rapidly" (Tickell)	The Jungle Owlet .	139
Loud resonant calls uttered when the bird is high up in the air	The Fish-Eagles	148-50
Peculiar squeaking wail uttered while the bird is sailing in the air	The Brahminy Kite	151
A mournful wailing trill, *chee-hĭ hĭ hĭ hĭ hĭ hĭ*, uttered on the wing	The Pariah Kite . .	152
A sharp double whistle . . .	The Shikra	158
A plaintive *cŭkoo-coo-coo* . .	The Spotted Dove .	166

Call	Name of Bird	No. of Bird in Part II
A soft subdued *cuk-cuk-coo-coo-coo*	The Little Brown Dove	167
Kŭ-kŭ—kū	The Indian Ring Dove	168
A deep grunting *coo-coo-coo*	The Red Turtle Dove	169
A loud *pe-haun,* rather like the *miau* of a cat	The Peafowl	170
A harsh, high-pitched, rapidly uttered *juk-juk, tee-tee-tur*	The Black Partridge	172
Three single harsh notes followed by a succession of shrill, ringing *pateela-pateela-pateelas*	The Grey Partridge	173
A very loud, hoarse, reiterated call, not easy to describe	The White-breasted Water-hen	174
Loud, penetrating, trumpet-like calls	The Cranes	177–179
Wild-sounding cry, heard at night	The Stone Curlew	180

Call	Name of Bird	No. of Bird in Part II
A loud, shrill "Did he do it? Pity to do it!"	The Red-wattled Lapwing	183
Like the above, but shorter .	The Yellow-wattled Lapwing . .	184
Clappering of the beak . . .	The Storks	216–221
A soft but penetrating *chakwa* or *á-onk* (Stuart Baker) . .	The Brahminy Duck	229

II. BIRDS WHOSE NESTS ARE LIKELY TO BE FOUND IN ANY GARDEN IN THE PLAINS

1. The Indian House Crow (3). (In tall trees.) (Also the Corby (1) in Madras.)
2. The Common Babbler (6). (In a bush; eggs blue.) (Not in Madras.)
3. One or other of the species of "Seven Sisters" (7–9). (In a bush; eggs blue.)
4. One or other of the Red-vented Bulbuls (15–18). (In a bush or plant growing in the

verandah ; eggs pale pink, blotched with reddish brown.)

5. One or other of the Red-whiskered Bulbuls (20 and 21). (Locally. Nest as in 4.)

6. The White-browed Bulbul (22). (In Madras only. Nest in bush, eggs as in 4.)

7. The King Crow (25). (Tiny cup in fork of tree.)

8. The Indian Tailor Bird (28). (In bush or plant growing in verandah. Two or three leaves stitched together.)

9. The Orioles (44 and 45). (In trees, very frequently quite close to that of a King Crow.)

10. The Brahminy Myna (51). (In hole in building.)

11. The Common Myna (52). (In hole in building or tree.)

12. The Pied Myna (54). (In low tree.) (Not in Punjab or S. India.)

13. The Indian Paradise Flycatcher (57). (In one of lower branches of tree.)

14. One or other of the Fantailed Flycatchers (58–60). (In a low tree or bush.)

15. The Brown Rock Chat (64). (*Inside* a building on a ledge.) (Not in S. India.)

16. The Indian Robins (66 and 67). (Very often on a window-sill.)

17. The Magpie Robin (68). (In hole in a wall or tree; eggs green with reddish blotches.)

18. The Yellow-throated Sparrow (81). (In hole in tree.)

19. The Common Sparrow (82). (Anywhere on the verandah or *inside* the bungalow.)

20. The Indian Pied Wagtail (92). (In hole in building.)

21. The Purple Sunbird (107). (Nest suspended from a bush or a rafter in the verandah.)

22. The Purple-rumped Sunbird (108). (Nest as in case of 21.)

23. The Golden-backed Woodpecker (111). (In hole in tree, which the bird hollows out.)

24. The Barbets (113 and 114). (In hole in tree, which the birds hollow out.)

25. The Indian Roller (115). (In hole in tree or building.)

26. The Indian Hoopoe (123). (In hole in tree or building.)

27. The Indian Swift (124). (In verandah or a deserted building.)

28. The Crow-Pheasant (131). (In a dense thicket.)

29. The Green Parrots (132–134). (In holes in trees; sometimes buildings.)

30. The Spotted Owlet (135). (In hole in tree or building.)

31. The Common Pariah Kite (152). (High up in tall trees.)

32. The Shikra (158). (In trees.)

33. The Doves (166–169). (In trees, and in the case of the Little Brown Dove often in the verandah.)

34. The Paddy Bird (224). (High up in tree.)

III. BIRDS THAT ARE FOND OF SITTING ON EXPOSED PERCHES, SUCH AS TELEGRAPH WIRES

1. The Crows (1–4).
2. The Drongos (25 and 26).
3. The Shrikes (34–37).
4. The Bush Chats (61–63).
5. The Common Sparrow (82).
6. The Swallows (88–90).
7. The Indian Roller (115).
8. The Bee-eaters (116 and 117).
9. The Kingfishers (118–120).
10. The White-eyed Buzzard (147).
11. The Doves (166–168).

IV. BIRDS WHICH ARE ALMOST INVARIABLY FOUND IN FLOCKS, EXCEPT WHEN NESTING

1. The Babblers (7–9). (Small flocks of seven or eight.)
2. The Indian White-eye (12).
3. The Nuthatches (23 and 24).
4. The Minivets (39–41). (Small flocks.)
5. The Cuckoo-Shrikes (42 and 43). (Small flocks.)
6. The Rose-coloured Starling (48). (Very large flocks.)
7. The Indian Starling (49).
8. The Grey-headed Myna (50). (Small flocks.) (The other species of Myna frequently, but by no means invariably, congregate in flocks.)
9. The Weaver Birds (70–73). (Small flocks.)
10. The Munias (74–79). (Especially the Red Munia.)
11. The Common Rose-Finch (80).
12. The Buntings (83–85). (Feed on the ripening grain.)
13. The Hornbills (121 and 122). (Small flocks.)

14. The Swifts (124 and 125).

15. The Green Parrots (132–134).

16. The Spotted Owlet (135). (Very small flocks ; probably family parties.)

17. The Vultures (141–143). (Only when feeding on a carcase.)

18. The Common Peafowl (170). (Small parties.)

19. The Common and Demoiselle Cranes (177 and 179). (The Saras Crane *never* goes in flocks.)

20. The Plovers (185 and 186).

21. The Little Stint (195).

22. The Indian Skimmer (206).

23. The Spoonbill (215).

24. The Cattle Egret (223).

25. The Night Heron (225).

26. The Common Flamingo (226).

27. The Geese (227 and 228).

28. The Shoveller (230).

29. Many of the Gulls and Terns go about in flocks.

V. FLIGHT

1. *Birds of very powerful flight,* i.e. *birds which spend a great part of the day on the wing*

1. The Swallows and Martins (86–90). (These live on small insects which they catch on the wing.)

2. The Swifts (124 and 125), (These feed in the same way as the swallows, but they *never* perch. When they wish to rest they go to their nests.)

3. The Pied Kingfisher (118). (This spends much of the day in fishing. It flies over the water and every now and again hovers on rapidly vibrating wings, and then drops on to its quarry in the water.)

4. The Osprey (140). (Obtains its food in much the same way as does the Pied Kingfisher.)

5. The Fishing Eagles (148–150).

6. The Brahminy Kite (151).

7. The common Pariah Kite (152). (These two species spend hours in the air sailing in circles looking out for their quarry.)

8. The Vultures (141–144). (These remain for hours high up in the air motionless on expanded wings, until one espies something to

eat on the earth below; it then descends, and its companions, observing this, follow suit.)

9. The Kestrel (162). (This behaves over land much as the Pied Kingfisher does over the water.)

10. The Gulls (196–199). (Everyone is familiar with the manner in which gulls follow ships.)

11. The Terns (200–206).

2. *Birds which make little sallies into the air from a perch after insects*

(*Vide* Feeding habits, 4.)

3. *Little birds which fly from the ground some twenty or thirty feet and then drop to the ground, singing as they descend*

The Finch-Larks (104 and 105).

VI. FEEDING HABITS

1. *Birds which feed largely on the ground*

1. The Crows (1–4). (These are omnivorous, and feed anywhere and everywhere.)

2. The Babblers (6–9).

3. The Malabar Whistling Thrush (11).

4. The Shrikes (34–37). (Descend from

perch to ground, seize their quarry, and return to perch and devour it.)

5. The Mynas (51–54).
6. The Bush Chats (61–63).
7. The Brown Rock Chats (64).
8. The Indian Redstart (65).
9. The Indian Robins (66 and 67).
10. The Magpie Robin (68).
11. The Munias (74–79).
12. The Wagtails (91–94).
13. The Pipits (95–96).
14. The Larks (97–105).
15. The Indian Pitta (109).
16. The Indian Roller (115). (Descends from perch to ground and seizes its quarry and then returns to perch.)
17. The Hoopoe (123).
18. The Crow-Pheasant (131).
19. The Vultures (141–145).
20. The Common Kite (152). (Drops from the air and seizes its food in its talons.)
21. The White-eyed Buzzard (147). (Swoops down from a perch on to a lizard, etc.)
22. The Harriers (153–157). (Fly low and drop on to their prey.)
23. The Kestrel (162). (Hovers on rapidly vibrating wings and drops on to its prey.)

24. The Blue Rock Pigeon (165).
25. The Doves (166–169).
26. All game and wading birds (except those that take their food off water).

2. *Birds that run up and down the trunks of trees, on which they find their food*

1. The Nuthatches (23 and 24).
2. The Woodpeckers (110 and 111).
3. The Common Wryneck (112).

3. *Birds that feed largely on insects which they pick off the foliage, sometimes hovering on vibrating wings in order to secure their quarry*

1. The Indian White-eye (12). (Frequents trees.)
2. The Tailor Bird (28). (Frequents bushes.)
3. The Warblers (29–32). (Frequent bushes.)
4. The Common Woodshrike (38). (Frequents trees).
5. The Minivets (39–41). (Frequent trees.)
6. The Cuckoo-Shrikes (42 and 43). (Frequent trees.)
7. The Sunbirds (106–108). (Frequent bushes.)

4. ***Birds which feed on insects which they catch in the air by making little sallies from a perch***

1. The Drongos (25 and 26).
2. The Flycatchers (55 and 60).
3. The Bee-eaters (116 and 117).

5. ***Birds which either catch fish or take their food off the surface of water***

1. The Kingfishers (118–120).
2. The Osprey (140).
3. The Fishing Eagles (148–150).
4. The Brahminy Kite (151).
5. The Gulls (196–199).
6. The Terns (200–205).
7. The Indian Skimmer (206).
8. The Pelicans (207 and 208).
9. The Cormorants (209–211).

VII. BIRDS WHICH HABITUALLY CARRY THE TAIL ALMOST VERTICALLY

1. The Tailor Bird (28).
2. The Indian Robins (66 and 67).
3. The Magpie Robin (68).

PART II

Descriptive List of the Common Birds of the Plains of India

DESCRIPTIVE LIST OF THE COMMON BIRDS OF THE PLAINS OF INDIA

NOTES

F. STANDS for ***The Fauna of British India,*** and the number which follows indicates the number of the bird in ***The Fauna of British India.*** J. stands for Jerdon's ***Birds of India,*** and the number that follows indicates the number of the bird in Jerdon's work.

In describing a bird its size is a matter of importance as an aid to identification ; but as the statement that a bird is six inches in length probably does not convey to the average person a definite idea of its size, I have adopted another system of indicating the size of each bird described. I have taken five standards of size, each being that of a familiar bird, and have described each species in terms of these standards, which are :

I. The common sparrow, 6 inches in length.
II. The bulbul, 8–9 inches in length.
III. The myna, 10 inches in length.
IV. The Indian house crow, 17½ ins. in length.
V. The kite, 23 inches in length.

My system is as follows. If A be a bird of which the length is 5 inches, I affix in a bracket – I, which means that is a bird smaller than a sparrow; if it be 6 inches in length I affix simply I; if it be 7 inches in length I affix + I, denoting that it is larger than a sparrow, but smaller than a bulbul, and nearer to the sparrow than the bulbul in dimensions; had its length been 7½ inches I should have described it as – II, i.e. rather smaller than a bulbul. By these means he who consults this book will at once be able to form a rough conception of the size of each species described. Those who desire more details will find them in *The Fauna of British India*. In this connection it is worthy of mention that certain small birds, as, for example, the adult cock paradise flycatcher, have very long tails. Such a bird, if measured from the tip of his beak to the end of his tail (as ornithologists usually do), would have to be described as – V, i.e. as a bird rather smaller than a kite, but this would convey a very misleading idea of the magnitude of the bird, the body of which is about the same size as that of the bulbul. I shall accordingly describe the paradise flycatcher as II, i.e. a bird of the same size as the bulbul, but shall note that the cock has a very long tail.

In cases where birds build very characteristic nests or have very characteristic songs or habits, I shall mention these as aids to identification. It must be remembered that this little book is not a natural history of birds, but merely a key to the identification of our commoner Indian feathered friends. Having identified a bird, the reader should refer to some other writer for information regarding its habits, etc.

In order to simplify identification I shall roughly indicate the distribution of each species. If nothing is said about the distribution of any bird this means that it may be found anywhere in the plains of India. If a species occurs in all parts save one or more the words " Not found in —— " will occur in the description. If the distribution be local, the description will contain the words " Found in ——."

As a further aid to identification I have, in all cases in which a species has been figured in any book which is easily procurable, stated where the picture of the bird is to be found. Most stations in India boast of a library of sorts, which is likely to contain some, at any rate, of the books referred to. In order to save space I have used abbreviations for the titles. Thus (Illus. F. I, p. 298) means that a picture of the bird in question will be found on page 298 of Volume I of the bird volume of *The Fauna of British India.*

List of abbreviations used

B. B. *The Common Birds of Bombay*, by Eha.
B. C. *The Birds of Calcutta* (2nd Edition), by Finn.
B. D. *Bombay Ducks*, by Dewar.
B. P. *Birds of the Plains*, by Dewar.
F. I. *Fauna of British India* (Birds, Vol. I).
F. II. Ditto, ditto, Vol. II.
F. III. Ditto, ditto, Vol. III.
F. IV. Ditto, ditto, Vol. IV.
G. B. *Garden and Aviary Birds of India*, by Finn.
I. F. *Some Indian Friends and Acquaintances*, by Cunningham.

I. D. *Indian Ducks and Their Allies*, by Stuart Baker.

I. G. I. *Game Birds of India, Burma, and Ceylon*, Vol. I., Marshall and Hume.

I. G. II. Ditto, ditto, ditto, Vol. II.

I. G. III. Ditto, ditto, ditto, Vol. III.

The Crows, 1–4

1. *Corvus macbrorbynchus:* The Jungle Crow or the Indian Corby. (F. 4), (J. 660), (+IV.)

Glossy black all over. Nests from March to May. Nest a large structure placed high up in a tree. Not found in the N.W. Punjab, where it is replaced by the next species. (Illus. B. D., p. 60; also B. B., p. 117, and I. F., p. 61.)

2. *Corvus corax:* The Raven. (F. I), (J. 657), (V.)

Glossy black all over. Found only in the N.W.F. province and the western parts of the Punjab.

3. *Corvus splendens:* The Indian House Crow, or the Grey-necked Crow. (F. 7), (J. 663), (IV.)

Like a jackdaw in marking and appearance. Glossy black, except for nape, neck, upper back and breast, which are ashy brown. (The hue of this ashy brown varies considerably with the locality, being lightest in the Punjab.) Nesting season May to July, or later. Nest like that of 1. In Burma this species is replaced by the next. (Illus. B. D., p. 168; also B. P., p. 190, and B. B., p. 117.)

4. *Corvus insolens:* The Burmese House Crow. (F. 8), (IV.)

A form of *C. splendens* in which the neck plumage is nearly as dark as that of the other parts.

5. *Dendrocitta rufa:* The Indian Tree-pie. (F. 16), (J. 674), (+II, but with tail a foot in length.)

Head, neck, and breast brownish black; body chestnut; silver-grey on the wings. Tail greyish with broad black band at the tip. During flight the tail assumes a curious shape owing to the fact that the feathers which compose it are graduated in length; the median pair is twelve inches long, the next pair is shorter, and so on, the outer pair being only about half the length of the median pair. This bird has a curious metallic call which may be syllabised· *coch-lee, coch-lee*, or *cogee, cogee.* It also emits a great variety of harsh cries. Breeds from April to August. The nest is a large cup high up in a tree.

(Does not appear to occur in or about the towns of Bombay and Madras.) (Illus. B. C., p. 10, but the illustration is not a good one, a better idea is given in F. I., p. 10, where an allied species is figured.)

The Babblers, 6–10

6. ***Argya caudata*:** The Common Babbler, or Striated Bush-babbler, or Rat-bird. (F. 105), (J. 438), (II.)

A dingy brown bird; upper plumage darker than the lower. In each feather there is a dark line along the shaft which causes the bird to have a streaked appearance. It goes about in pairs, or in small flocks. It feeds largely on the ground. When it runs, its tail (which is about 4½ inches long, i.e. half the total length of the bird) seems to trail on the ground like that of a rat, hence one of its names. Its note is not unpleasant. It nests chiefly in the hot weather. The nursery is a neatly constructed cup, which is invariably placed in a low bush. Its eggs are pale blue.

Does not appear to occur in the neighbourhood of Calcutta, Bombay, or Madras. Addicted to arid parts of India.

7–9. *The Crateropus Babblers, or "Seven Sisters."*

These are all untidy-looking, earthy-brown birds about the size of mynas. They go about in little flocks, whence the name "Seven Sisters," or "*Sath Bhai.*" They feed largely on the ground, seeking for insects among dead leaves. While feeding they keep up a constant chatter which every now and then grows very loud, sounding like a combination of a squeak and the groans of a revolving axle that requires to be oiled. They continually jerk the tail, which has the appearance of being very loosely inserted. So untidy-looking are these birds that Eha likens them to "Old Jones, who spends the day in his pyjamas." Their flight is feeble and laborious. Three species are common :

7. *Crateropus canorus :* The Jungle Babbler. (F. 110), (J. 432), (III.)

This bird is abundant in Northern India, and becomes rarer in the south, where it is largely replaced in the plains by the two next species. (Illus. B. C., p. 15.)*

* At Allahabad the Large Grey Babbler (*Argya malcomi*) (F. 107), or *Gangai*, is more abundant even than *C. canorus*. It may be recognised by its long tail.

8. *Crateropus griseus:* The White-headed Babbler. (F. 111), (J. 433), (III.)

This is the common babbler of the Madras presidency. It is easily recognised by the greyish white crown of its head. (Illus. B. D., p. 204.)

9. *Crateropus somervillii:* The Rufous-tailed Babbler. (F. 113) (J. 435), (III.)

The common babbler of Bombay and Poona. It is the least untidy-looking of the babblers, and may be recognised by the distinctly reddish hue of its tail.

All three species of babblers build neat cup-shaped nests not far above the ground and lay beautiful blue eggs. (Illus. B. B., p. 80.)

10. *Pyctorhis sinensis:* The Yellow-eyed Babbler. (F. 139), (J. 385), (+I.)

This is considerably smaller than the other babblers described. Its general colour is cinnamon brown. The eyebrows, throat, and breast are white. The under parts are cream-coloured. The eye is bright yellow. It emits a sweet note and builds a beautiful nest. This last is in shape not unlike the hat worn by a political officer in full dress. It measures about five inches in depth and is usually slung by its broadest part on to two or more growing reeds, heads of millet, stout grass stems, or perhaps more frequently to a forked branch.

11. *Myiophoneus horsfieldi* : The Malabar Whistling Thrush, or Idle Schoolboy. (F. 189), (J. 342), (+III.)

A black bird with large cobalt blue patches on the forehead and the wings. Small patches of the same hue occur on other parts of the body.

Not found in the N.W. Frontier Province, the Punjab, United Provinces, Bengal, or the eastern portion of Madras. Usually occurs in the neighbourhood of shaded streams. Its note is a striking whistle.

12. *Zosterops palpebrosa* : The Indian White-eye, or Spectacle Bird. (F. 226), (J. 631), (– I.)

A greenish yellow bird, with bright yellow throat and a patch of yellow under the tail. The rest of the lower plumage is greyish white. The most noticeable feature of the bird is a ring of white feathers round the eye. Hence its popular name. White-eyes go about in large flocks ; they feed largely on insects which they pick from off the leaves of trees. Each individual utters unceasingly a cheeping note. At the nesting season, which is usually at the beginning of the hot weather, the cock sings a sweet little song. The nest is a beautiful little cup suspended from a forked branch. Two pale blue egges are usually laid. (Illus. G. B., p. 96.)

13. *Ægithina tiphia:* The Common Iora. (F. 243), (J. 468), (– I.)

Cock: (*a*) In summer upper plumage, wings, and tail are black; lower parts bright yellow. There are two white bars in the wing.

(*b*) In winter the black parts of the head and back are replaced by yellowish green.

Hen: Upper parts, wings, and tail green; lower parts yellow. Two white bars in the wing.

This species has a sweet song. It does not occur in the Frontier Province or the Punjab. "A little bird," writes Eha, "like a tomtit, in black and yellow, followed by its mate in green and yellow, can be nothing else than the Iora." Builds at the beginning of the hot weather a very neat and tiny cup-shaped nest. (Illus. B. B., p. 91, also G. B., p. 64.)

The Bulbuls, 14–22

14. *Chloropsis Jerdoni*. The Common Green Bulbul, or Jerdon's Chloropsis. (F. 252), (J. 463), (– II.)

A beautiful emerald green bird. There is a patch of yellow on the forehead. The cock has the sides of the head, chin, and throat black, and a purple-blue moustache. The black of the male is replaced by bluish green in the hen.

Does not occur in the Frontier Province, the Punjab, Rajputana, Bengal, or the northern and western portions of the United Provinces. It is essentially a bird of Central and Southern India, but rare on the east coast. It affects well-wooded parts of the country. (Illus. G. B., p. 96.)

The Red-vented Bulbuls, 15–18

Head black with short crest; remainder of plumage brown, each feather having a narrow margin of a lighter hue. The tail is tipped with white, and there is a white patch above the tail. A conspicuous crimson patch under the tail. Bulbuls go about in pairs and constantly emit a cheery note. They build neat cup-shaped nests, frequently in plants in the verandahs of houses. When the nest is approached by a human being the parent birds set up a loud chattering. These bulbuls occur all over India, but ornithologists divide them into several species :

15. *Molpastes hæmorrhous :* The Madras Red-vented Bulbul. (F. 278), (J. 462), (II.)

The common bulbul of South India, as far North as Lucknow. (Illus. B. D., p. 296; also B. B., p. 87.)

16. *Molpastes burmanicus :* The Burmese Red-vented Bulbul. (F. 279), (II.)

The common bulbul of Burma.

17. *Molpastes bengalensis :* The Bengal Red-vented Bulbul. (F. 282), (J. 461), (II.)

The common bulbul of Eastern Oudh, the Bengals, and Assam. (Illus. B. C., p. 22.)

18. *Molpastes intermedius :* The Punjab Red-vented Bulbul. (F. 283), (J. II., p. 95) (II.)

The common bulbul of the Frontier Province, the Punjab, and the province of Agra.

[At the points where the various species or races of red-vented bulbuls meet they interbreed, so that at Lucknow and other points of junction it is not possible to assign the local bulbuls to any of the above species.]

19. *Molpastes leucotis :* The White-eared Bulbul. (F. 285), (J. 459), (– II.)

This species differs from the Red-vented Bulbuls in its somewhat smaller size, its shorter crest and in having a large white patch on each side of the head, and the patch of feathers under the tail yellow instead of crimson.

Found only in the north-west portion of India. In the cold weather its range extends into the Province of Agra and the C. P., but in the spring it migrates to the west and breeds in Sind, the Frontier Province, and the Western Districts of the Punjab. Its nests have also been taken in Rajputana, Katywar, and Cutch. (Illus. G. B., p. 96; also F. I., p. 252.)

The Red-whiskered Bulbuls, 20 *and* 21

These sprightly and handsome birds are characterised by their long crests, which end in a point and project forward, like Mr. Punch's cap. The head and crest are black, but each cheek is characterised by a large white and a small crimson patch, hence the name "red-whiskered." The upper plumage is earthy brown. The tail feathers are somewhat darker brown and are tipped with white. The breast and lower plumage are white. The breast is separated from the abdomen by a conspicuous band of black feathers known as the collaret. There is a crimson patch of feathers under the tail.

20. *Otocompsa emeria:* The Bengal Red-whiskered Bulbul. (F. 288), (J. 460), (II.)

Found in Northern and Eastern India, and Burma. (Illus. B. P., p. 230; also B. C., p. 26.)

21. *Otocompsa fuscicaudata:* The Southern Red-whiskered Bulbul. (F. 289), (J. 460), (II.)

Found chiefly in the south-western portion of India, more especially in the hills. This is the common bulbul of all our South-Indian hill stations.

This species is distinguishable from *Emeria* in that it has a complete collaret. In *Emeria* the black collaret is interrupted in front.

Both the *Molpastes* and the *Otocompsa* bulbuls build neat cup-shaped nests in trees and shrubs in gardens. Not infrequently they nest in plants growing in pots placed in the verandah. (Illus. B. D., p. 296; also B. B., p. 87.)

22. *Pycnonotus luteolus:* The White-browed Bulbul. (F. 305), (J. 452), (–II.)

A dull greenish brown bird, having no crest.

It has a white eyebrow, and the patch of feathers under the tail is pale yellow.

It occurs only in Southern India and is exceedingly common in the vicinity of Madras. It frequents gardens and utters a variety of very cheery little notes, and has, therefore, been called "the blithest little bird in existence." It does not show itself very much in the open, being heard much more frequently than seen. It builds a cup-shaped nest in a bush or low tree.

The Nuthatches, 23 and 24

Nuthatches are little climbing birds characterised by very short tails. They go about in small flocks and run up and down the trunks and branches of trees with great address, picking up small insects. They also, as their name implies, feed upon nuts. They nest in holes of trees, frequently closing up a portion of the aperture with mud. (Illus. F. I., p. 298.)

23. *Sitta castaneiventris:* The Chestnut-bellied Nuthatch. (F. 321), (J. 250), (– I.)

Upper plumage dark greyish blue. A broad black band runs from the beak, through the eye and down the side of the head. The other parts of the cheek are white. The lower plumage is dark chestnut-red, as denoted by the popular name of the bird. (The lower parts of the hen are of a lighter hue.) Distribution : U. P., C. P., C. I., and western parts of Bengal.

24. *Sitta frontalis :* The Velvet-fronted Blue Nuthatch. (F. 325), (J. 253), (– I.)

Upper plumage dark blue, the cock having a velvet-like black forehead and a black streak through the eye ; throat whitish ; lower parts greyish.

Not found in the Punjab.

The Drongos, 25–27

25. *Dicrurus ater :* The Black Drongo, or King Crow. (F. 327), (J. 278), (II, but with a tail six inches long.)

Jet black all over, with a long-forked tail. One of the most familiar of Indian birds. It frequently perches on telegraph wires, or on the backs of cattle. It makes little flights after insects and then returns to its perch. Its call is very cheery and is heard most often at earliest dawn.

It breeds in the hot weather ; the nest is a small cup, wedged into the fork of a lofty branch. The oriole and the dove frequently nest in the same tree.

Found all over India, but only a summer visitor to the Frontier Province and the Western Punjab, and a winter visitor to Assam. (Illus. B. D., frontispiece; also I. F., p. 148, and B. B., p. 1.)

26. *Dicrurus cærulescens:* The White-bellied Drongo. (F. 330), (J. 281), (II, but with long-forked tail.)

Very like the King Crow (No. 25) in appearance, save that it is a little smaller and its plumage is deep indigo instead of glossy black (but it looks black from a distance). The breast is grey and the abdomen white.

This bird, although nowhere common in India, is found in all parts save the N.W. F. P., the Punjab, and the eastern portion of Bengal.

27. *Dissemurus paradiseus:* The Larger Racket-tailed Drongo. (F. 339), (J. 284), (II, but with a tail 20 inches long.)

Glossy black all over. The head is decorated by a large backwardly-directed crest. The two outer tail feathers are a foot and a half in length; on the inner side of the shaft there is scarcely any web, while the web on the outer shaft grows longer as it nears the tip of the feather. These elongated outer feathers are turned upwards and outwards at the tip.

Confined almost entirely to forests, and hence is very rarely seen in the plains.

The Warblers, 28–33

28. *Orthotomus sutorius:* The Indian Tailor Bird. (F. 374), (J. 530), (– I.)

A tiny brownie bird not unlike a wren with a respectable tail. Close inspection shows that the forehead is reddish, the back of the head grey, and the back brown, tinged with green. The lower plumage is dirty creamy white. There is a short black bar on each side of the neck, visible only when the bird stretches its neck to utter its note, but as the bird is continually calling loudly *to-wee, to-wee, to-wee*, a little watching will soon reveal the black patch on the side of the neck.

In the hot weather the two middle tail feathers of the cock exceed the others in length by fully two inches. These projecting, bristle-like tail feathers render it very easy to recognise the cock tailor bird in breeding plumage.

The tailor bird is essentially a denizen of the compound, and frequently nests in the verandah. The nest is a wonderful structure. The walls are growing leaves, the edges of which the bird draws together by means of cotton or fibre. The nest is cosily lined with cotton-down. The tailor bird pierces in places the leafy wall of its nest and pushes some of the lining through these tiny apertures in order to keep the lining *in situ*. The nest should be looked for in the hot weather. (Illus. B. B., p. 103; also G. B., p. 64.)

29. *Hypolais rama:* Sykes's Tree-warbler. (F. 394), (J. 553), (– I.)

This, too, is a dull-coloured little brownie bird. It visits India in great numbers in the winter, and is said to breed in Sind. In colouring it is much like the tailor bird, but it is more solidly built and has a narrow cream-coloured eyebrow. A little brown bird which is not the tailor bird, or one of the wren-warblers described below, is likely to be this species.

30. *Prinia lepida:* The Streaked Wren-warbler. (F. 462), (J. 550), (– I.)

Brown above and cream-coloured below. This little bird is easily distinguished from the other long-tailed wrens, by the fact that its upper plumage is streaked with dark brown. The brown tail shows cross bars. The tip of each tail feather is white and next to this is a black patch.

This bird is common in the Punjab and in Sind. It also occurs in Rajputana and in the valley of the Ganges.

It builds a neat ball-like nest with an entrance at the side. The nest is usually situated at a few inches from the ground. Several are to be found in April and May amid the wild indigo that grows on the Lahore golf links. The green eggs have a distinct ring of reddish dots at the thick end.

31. *Prinia socialis:* The Ashy Wren-warbler. (F. 464), (J. 534), (–I.)

Another "tiny brownie bird." Ashy upper plumage with brown wings and tail, lower plumage cream-coloured. A very slender and loosely-knit bird. It is easily distinguished by the curious snapping noise it makes as it flits from bush to bush. How this noise is made we do not know. It sounds as though it were due to the upper and lower mandibles of the beak closing sharply together.

This species constructs two types of nests—

one is like that of the Tailor Bird (No. 28), the other is a ball-like woven structure with an entrance at the side. The nest is invariably placed near the ground. The eggs are mahogany red. Does not occur in the N.W. F. P.

32. ***Prinia inornata:*** The Indian Wren-warbler. This bird is known as the weaver-bird to boys who attend Indian schools. (F. 466), (J. 543), (– I.)

This species differs so little in appearance from the last that except for the snapping noise it is almost impossible to distinguish them unless held in the hand and compared. This species has rusty-coloured thighs, and these may serve to distinguish it from the last species.

It builds a nicely-woven ball-like nest, which is frequently attached to growing corn, and the parent birds sometimes have their work cut out in rearing up their brood before the crop is cut. Eggs greenish with red and brown blotches.

Found in N. India. At the Nilgiris this species meets the next.

33. ***Prinia Jerdoni:*** The Southern Wren-warbler. (F. 467), (J. 544), (– I.)

This is the South Indian form of No. 32,

and has very much the same habits and appearance as the last species. (Illus. B. B., p. 103.)

The Shrikes, or Butcher Birds, 34–37

The shrikes form a well-marked family of birds. Their habit is to sit on an exposed perch and from thence pounce on to some insect on the ground. Thus their habits are like those of some birds of prey. Their hooked and notched beaks and the broad black band that runs from the base of the beak through the eye gives them a very sinister appearance. They have a variety of notes.

34. *Lanius lahtora :* The Indian Grey Shrike (F. 469), (J. 256), (+II.)

Upper parts French grey ; forehead black ; broad black band from base of beak, through eye and down the side of the neck. Tail black and white ; wings black with conspicuous white bar. Breast and lower plumage white.

Sind, Punjab, U. P., C. P., and Western Bengal.

The nest of this and of the other species of butcher bird is a deep cup, placed usually in a thorny tree, often close up against the trunk. Not infrequently bits of rag hang down from the nest and serve to locate its whereabouts. The eggs have a stone-coloured background with brownish blotches, which often form a ring near the large end. (Illus. B. B., p. 70; also F. I., p. 454.)

35. *Lanius vittatus*: The Bay-backed Shrike. (F. 473), (J. 260), (– II.)

Forehead and broad band through the eye black. Head pale grey, back maroon, rump white; wings black with a white bar, which is conspicuous during flight. Tail black and white, median feathers black, outer ones white; lower parts white with a reddish-yellow tinge on the breast.

36. *Lanius erythronotus*: The Rufous-backed Shrike. (F. 476), (J. 257), (+II.)

Although smaller than the last species, this bird is very like it in colouring. It may, however, be distinguished by the fact that it has no white in the tail. The rump is the same colour as the upper back and not white as in 35.

37. *Lanius cristatus*: The Brown Shrike. (F. 481), (J. 261), (– II.)

This species is distinguishable from the above three shrikes by the fact that it lacks the white wing bar which makes the others so conspicuous during flight. A reddish-brown bird with white cheeks and throat and a whitish eyebrow.

Unlike the other butcher birds this species is merely a winter visitor to India. It spreads itself over all parts of the country save the N.W. F. P. and the Punjab. (A few individuals are said to remain in India to nest.)

It has a harsh chattering note, which it utters incessantly. It is regarded in Calcutta as the herald of the cold weather. (Illus. G. B., p. 16.)

38. *Tephrodornis pondicerianus:* The Common Woodshrike. (F. 488), (J. 265), (+I.)

An ashy-brown bird, having a broad white eyebrow and the outer tail feathers white. Occurs chiefly in gardens and avenues. It is most easily recognised by its pretty mellow note, which Jesse syllabises as *tanti-tuia*.

The Minivets, 39–41

Minivets are brightly coloured little birds, which usually go about in small flocks, picking insects from off the leaves of trees. They build neat cup-shaped nests, which are usually placed on a horizontal branch. The nest is difficult to find, as when seen from below it looks like a knot in the branch. The flocks lead a wandering existence.

39. *Pericrocotus speciosus :* The Indian Scarlet Minivet. (F. 490), (J. 271), (I, but with tail of 4½ inches long.)

Cock : A beautiful bird arrayed in bright scarlet and black. The head and shoulders are black, the back and lower parts scarlet. The wings are black with a scarlet bar running along (and not, as is usual, across) the wing. Tail feathers scarlet except the median pair, which are black.

Hen : Head and body bright yellow, wings black with longitudinal yellow bar. Tail yellow and black.

Occurs in U. P., Bengal, Assam, and C. P.

40. *Pericrocotus brevirostris :* The short-billed Minivet. (F. 495), (J. 273), (– I, but with tail 4 inches long.)

Very much like the Scarlet Minivet (39) in appearance, save that the red of the cock is crimson rather than scarlet.

Occurs in Punjab, Rajputana, U. P., Bengal, Assam and C. P. (Illus. G. B., p. 64.)

41. *Pericrocotus peregrinus :* The Small Minivet. (F. 500), (J. 276), (– I, tail 3 inches long.)

Cock: Head and shoulders slaty grey, lower back deep scarlet, wings black with red bar, tail black with red at tip, chin and throat blackish, breast scarlet; lower plumage orange-yellow.

Hen: Upper parts grey, lower parts creamy white, wing brown with yellow or orange wing-bar, tail black with red tip.

Not found in the N.W. F. P.

The Cuckoo-Shrikes, 42 *and* 43

42. *Campephaga sykesi:* The Black-headed Cuckoo-Shrike. (F. 508), (J. 268), (– II.)

Cock: Head, throat, and breast black; rest of plumage grey shading into white on the abdomen; tail black with broad white tip.

Hen: Upper parts grey, lower parts whitish with narrow black cross bars, tail as in cock. This species goes about in small flocks, is strictly arboreal, and has many of the habits of the minivets.

Not found in Punjab or N.W. F. P.

43. *Graucalus macii:* The Large Cuckoo-Shrike. (F. 510), (J. 270), (+ III.)

A large pale slaty-grey bird with a black patch in front of the eye. The lower parts are paler than the upper parts and often exhibit more or less distinct narrow black cross bars ; habits as above.

Found all over India, but rare in the N.W. portion of the peninsula.

Neither 42 or 43 are very common birds.

The Orioles, 44 *and* 45

44. *Oriolus kundoo :* The Indian Oriole, or Mango Bird. (F. 518), (J. 470), (– III.)

Cock : A bright yellow bird with a pink beak and red eyes. There is some black on the sides of the head and in the wings and the tail. During flight this bird looks like a flash of gold.

Hen : Of duller hue than the cock, with greenish back.

A strictly arboreal species. The note is a soft, rich, mellow *peeho, peeho.*

The nest is a wonderful structure—a large cup slung like a hammock or prawn net on the fork of a bow, usually placed in one of the lower branches of a lofty tree, but out of reach of a human being. This species very frequently builds in the same tree as the King Crow. The eggs are pale pink, with chocolate blotches, which wash off.

This bird is not found in Eastern Bengal, or in the eastern portion of Bengal proper. It is found all the year round in most parts of India, but is merely a summer visitor to the Punjab, N.W. F. P., and the Himalayas.

45. *Oriolus melanocephalus:* The Black-headed Oriole. (F. 521), (J. 472 and 473), (– III.)

Very much like the last species, but is distinguishable by having the whole head, chin, throat, and upper breast black.

Not found in the Punjab, or N.W. F. P., or in the Himalayas. (Illus. G. B., p. 16; also I. F., p. 128.)

The Grackles, or Hill Mynas, 46 *and* 47

As these birds are almost exclusively confined to hilly and well-wooded regions they can scarcely be numbered among the common birds of the plains of India; but as they are so very frequently seen in cages, I mention them.

They are larger than the common myna, but have a much shorter tail. They are glossy black birds with a conspicuous white wing bar. Beak orange-yellow, legs pale yellow. Their most conspicuous feature is the pair of yellow wattles.

46. *Eulabes religiosa:* The Southern Grackle. (F. 523), (J. 692), (III.)

Found only in S. India.

47. *Eulabes intermedia:* The Indian Grackle. (F. 524), (J. 693), (+III.)

Found in the Himalayas and C. P.

The Starlings, 48–54

48. *Pastor roseus:* The Rose-coloured Starling, or Jowaree Bird, or Tilyer. (F. 528), (J. 690), (+III.)

Cock: Head, throat, wings, and tail glossy black; rest of plumage rose-coloured pink.

Hens and young cocks: In these the pink is replaced by a pinkish grey, or pale coffee-coloured hue. The great majority of birds one sees in India are hens or young cocks. The head is crested, but the black crest rests flat on the head, so that it is not noticeable.

Rosy starlings do not breed in India, although individuals may be seen in all months of the year. The birds are most abundant in the winter. Preparatory to leaving the country for breeding purposes rosy starlings congregate in huge flocks in April and May. These flocks do much damage to the grain, and hence are known as *Jowaree* and *Cholum* birds. They are also very partial to mulberries, and are therefore sometimes known as Mulberry birds. (B. D., p. 86.)

49. *Sturnus menzbieri :* The Common Indian Starling. (F. 532), (J. 681), (+II.)

Very like the common English starling in appearance. Glossy black with numbers of small yellow or buff spots ; in certain lights it shows a green or bronze sheen.

A winter visitor to Northern India. Abundant in the Punjab during the cold weather, where it is usually seen in flocks.

50. *Sturnia malabarica :* The Grey-headed Myna. (F. 538), (J. 688), (II.)

Head pale grey, chin almost white, rest of upper plumage dark grey with a reddish tinge, throat and breast reddish grey with a white shaft to each feather ; remainder of lower plumage rusty red. Beak greenish blue with yellow tip.

Not found in Sind, N.W. F. P., or the Punjab. In the other parts of India it undergoes local migration. I have seen it in Madras only in the cold weather.

This is the most arboreal of the mynas, rarely if ever descending to the ground, and frequenting the topmost branches of trees. It associates in small flocks. Its note is a harsh chuckle.

51. *Temenuchus pagodarum:* The Black-headed or Brahminy Myna, or Pawai. (F. 544), (J. 687), (+II.)

Head, neck, and lower plumage rich buff; wings black and grey; tail feathers brown with white tips; head and crest black. The long crest rests flat on the neck and looks like a pig-tail, having a silky hair-like appearance. Beak blue with yellow tip. Legs bright yellow.

Like most other mynas this species nests in a hole. In this case the nest-hole is usually in some building or tree. An unpleasant odour emanates from the nest.

This bird and No. 50 are very alike in shape and colouring, the most noticeable difference being in the colour of the head and crest and of the legs.

Not found in Eastern Bengal, the N.W. F. P., or the western portion of the Punjab. (Illus. B. D., p. 82; also B. B., p. 124.)

52. *Acridotheres tristis:* The Common Myna. (F. 549), (J. 684), (III.)

One of the most familiar of our Indian birds. Head, neck, and upper breast black; rest of body plumage rich brown; wings black, showing a very conspicuous white bar during flight. Tail feathers black with broad white tips, visible during flight. Beak and legs bright yellow; bright yellow patch of skin behind eye.

This bird is found in every garden in India. It feeds largely on the ground.

It is a noisy bird. Eha describes its notes as "*Keeky, keeky, keeky . . . churr, churr, kok, kok, kok.* Each time it says *kok* it points to the ground with its beak and bobs its head." (Illus. B. D., p. 84; also F. I., p. 516, and B. C., p. 44.)

53. *Acridotheres ginginianus:* The Bank or Well Myna. (F. 551), (J. 685), (– III.)

Very like 51 in shape, but its prevailing tint is grey instead of brown. The wing bar and the tips of the tail feathers are buff instead of white, and the patch of skin behind the eye is crimson instead of yellow.

Not found in S. India.

It goes about in flocks and nests in holes in river banks or wells, hence its popular name.

54. *Sturnopastor contra.* The Pied Myna. (F. 555), (J. 683), (– III.)

A black bird, white cheeks and rump, and white bar at base of wing; lower parts grey. Beak orange with white tip; orange patch of skin behind the eye.

This bird differs from the other mynas in that it builds a large nest in a tree, usually at no great altitude.

Occurs only in U. P., C. P., the Bengals, and Assam. (Illus. G. B., p. 16.)

The Flycatchers, 55–60

Flycatchers are birds which feed exclusively on insects, which they catch upon the wing. Their habit is to make, from some perch, little sallies into the air after their quarry. It must, however, not be forgotten that birds other than flycatchers, as, for example, the king crow and the wagtails, also hunt for insects in this manner; so that it is not safe to set down a bird as a flycatcher merely because it makes little sallies into the air after insect quarry.

A considerable number of species of flycatcher occur in India, but the great majority of them are confined to the hills. The following, however, are likely to be seen in the plains, Nos. 57–60 being especially abundant.

55. *Alseonax latirostris.* The Brown Flycatcher. (F. 588), (J. 297), (– I.)

An ashy-brown bird; tail darker than body, lower parts white, inconspicuous ring of white feathers round the eye. Not a very common bird.

Not found in N.W. F. P., Punjab, Sind, or Rajputana.

A little brown bird with a short tail, that makes a sally into the air after an insect, and then returns to its perch, is probably this species.

56. *Culicicapa ceylonensis:* The Grey-headed Flycatcher. (F. 592), (J. 295), (– I.)

Head, neck, and breast ash-coloured. Back greenish yellow; wings and tail dark brown. Lower plumage dull yellow.

A rare bird in the plains. Not likely to be seen in N.W. India.

57. *Terspiphone paradisi:* The Indian Paradise Flycatcher, also known as the Ribbon Bird and the Widow Bird. (F. 598), (J. 288), (II, but the cock has a very long tail.)

One of the most beautiful birds in India.

Hen and young cock: Like a bulbul in size and form. Rich chestnut plumage with metallic black crest and head; lower parts white. Bill bluish black. Legs slate-coloured.

Second year cock: Similar to above, except that the two median tail feathers are much longer than the others, being 16 inches in length.

Old cocks: The chestnut parts of the plumage turn white.

This bird undergoes a certain amount of local migration. It visits the Punjab in great numbers in summer for nesting purposes. The nest is like an inverted cone in shape, and is usually placed on one of the lower branches of a tree. The white cock shares the duties of incubation, and as he sits, his long white tail feathers hang down several inches beyond the bottom of the nest.

The bird frequently utters a sharp note something like the twitter of a sparrow. The cock has also a sweet little song.

In Burma this species is replaced by an allied species—the Burmese Paradise Flycatcher (*T. affinis*). (Illus. F. II., p. 1; also B. B., p. 76, and G. B. frontispiece.)

The Fantail Flycatchers, 58–60

These are blackish-brown birds, with a conspicuous white eyebrow. There are some white spots in the wing. The tail feathers are tipped with white, and as the bird continually spreads its tail into a fan the white is very conspicuous. The lower plumage is white. These birds have a striking and very cheery song of about six notes, which they utter constantly. They are easily recognised by their "tinkling" song and by the manner in which they continually fan the tail, drop the wings, and dance; or, to use Eha's words, "waltz and pirouette among the lower branches of a shady mango tree." Three species are common, and have similar manners and appearance. The nest is either a neat cup or an inverted cone, built largely of cobweb on one of the lower branches of a tree. When they have a nest these flycatchers are very bold. They will set upon and drive away birds much larger than themselves, and will even offer to attack an intruding human being. The three species are distinguished as follows:

58. *Rhipidura albifrontata:* The white-browed Fantail Flycatcher. (F. 604), (J. 292), (+I.)

Distinguished by its very broad white eye-brow and forehead. The common species of N. India. Nest a cup.

59. *Rhipidura albicollis:* The White-throated Fantail Flycatcher. (F. 605), (J. 291), (+I.)

Distinguished from 58 by the black forehead and narrow white eyebrow, and from 60 by the black abdomen. Nest an inverted cone. The common fantail of S. and E. India.

60. *Rhipidura pectoralis:* The White-spotted Fantail Flycatcher (F. 607), (J. 293), (+I.)

Distinguished from 58 by the black forehead and narrow white eyebrow, and from 59 by the whitish abdomen. Nest cup-shaped. The common fantail of S.W. India. (Illus. B. B., p. 76.)

The Robins, 61–69

61 and 62. *The Pied Bush Chats.*

The *cock* is a black bird (brownish in early winter), with a conspicuous white wing patch and a white rump.

The *hen* is a reddish-brown bird (greyish in winter), with a black tail with a reddish patch over the tail. The hen may be distinguished from other brownish birds by the peculiar colouring of her mate.

The nest is in a hole in the ground at the base of a tussock of long grass.

61. *Pratincola caprata:* The Common Pied

Bush Chat, or White-winged Black Robin. (F. 608), (J. 481), (– I.)

Found in N. and C. India.

62. *Pratincola atrata:* The Southern Pied Bush Chat. (F. 609), (J. 482), (I.)

Found in S. India.

The above two species may perhaps be regarded as local varieties.

63. *Pratincola maura:* The Indian Bush Chat. (F. 610), (J. 483), (– I.)

Cock: The upper parts are reddish brown in winter (black in summer owing to the brown edges to the feathers being worn away). Large patch of white on each side of neck; breast orange-red, lower parts pale reddish brown.

Hen: Reddish brown all over; no white neck patch.

A winter visitor to all parts of Northern India; occurs usually in open fields.

The hens of these species of robin-like birds are very difficult to distinguish; but as they are usually found in company with the cock it is not as a rule difficult to assign them to their proper species.

64. *Cercomela fusca:* The Brown Rock Chat—the *Desi shama* of Indians. (F. 629), (J. 494), (+I.)

A dull inconspicuous brown bird. It frequents buildings and is robin-like in its habits. As it hops about it continually bobs its head. The cock sings a sweet little lay. The nest is made up of dried grass and placed in a niche or on a ledge in an outhouse, or a mosque, or even an inhabited room. It is made of dried grass and roots, and falls to pieces if lifted from its foundation. The eggs are pale blue blotched with reddish yellow.

Found in Punjab, Rajputana, U. P., and C. P.; very common at Lahore.

65. *Ruticilla rufiventris:* The Indian Redstart. (F. 644), (J. 497), (I.)

Cock: Each feather of the head, breast, and upper plumage is black, fringed with grey, so that after the autumn moult the cock is dark grey in these parts; but gradually the grey edges wear away, so that by the spring the head, neck, and upper parts of the cock look black. The rump and the feathers over the tail are reddish chestnut. The abdomen is orange-red. All the feathers of the tail are reddish except the two median ones, which are brown.

Hen: Reddish brown when the cock is grey or black; otherwise like the cock, except that the red in her plumage is duller.

The redstart is an easy bird to identify, it behaves as though it had St. Vitus' dance in the tail. As it flies away all the red in its plumage shows, so that the bird looks like a ball of fire. It feeds largely on the ground, taking cover in bushes when alarmed. It frequents gardens.

A winter visitor to India. Very common in the north and rarer in the south.

66. *Thamnobia cambaiensis:* The Brown-backed Indian Robin. (F. 661), (J. 480), (+I.)

Cock: A glossy black bird with a brown back, a narrow white bar in the wing, and a conspicuous patch of brick-red under the tail.

Hen: A sandy brown bird with a brick-red patch under the tail.

A familiar bird which haunts gardens and is very partial to dry sandy localities. It builds a neat cup-shaped nest on window-ledges or in holes in walls, banks, etc. It usually carries the tail raised almost vertically and so displays the red patch. Occurs all over Northern India. South of the Godaveri it is replaced by 67.

67. *Thamnobia fulicata:* The Black-backed Indian Robin. (F. 662), (J. 479), (+I.)

The hen of this species is scarcely distinguishable from the hen of *T. cambaiensis* (66). The cock differs in having the back black instead of brown. Occurs only in S. India. (Illus. B. D., p. 294.)

68. *Copsychus saularis:* The Magpie Robin, or Dayal. (F. 663), (J. 475), (– II.)

A very familiar garden bird.

Cock: A glossy black bird, with a white abdomen sharply marked off from the black throat and breast. Outer tail feathers white. A conspicuous white wing bar.

Hen: Marked like the cock, but greyish brown where he is black. This species, like the last, frequently elevates the tail.

The cock has a fine song in spring. This and the magpie pattern of its plumage cause it to be readily identified. The cock and hen pair for life. They frequent gardens and are robin-like in habits. It nests in holes in trees or buildings. The nest is frequently found in stables and outhouses. (Illus. F. II., p. 56; also G. B., frontispiece, and B. B., p. 97.)

69. *Cittocincla macrura:* The Shama. (F. 664), (J. 476), (II, but with a tail six inches long.)

A fine songster.

Cock: Upper plumage glossy black. Lower

back white. Wings black and white. Lower plumage chestnut red.

Hen: Like the cock, save that the black is replaced by slaty brown and the reddish lower parts are much paler than in the cock.

Found only in thick jungle. (Illus. G. B., p. 40.)

The Weaver Birds, 70–73

Weaver birds are sparrow-like birds of gregarious habits. They build, or rather weave, wonderful flask-shaped or retort-shaped nests which hang from trees, the entrance being from below. They breed in the rains. Four species are found in India, these are:

70. *Ploceus baya:* The Baya, or Common Weaver Bird, or Bottle Bird. (F. 720), (J. 694), (I.)

At most seasons of the year the cock and hen are reddish-brown birds with a faint, fawn-coloured eyebrow, and look very like the hen house sparrow, having, like her, a thick bill. The hen baya retains this plumage throughout the year. In the hot weather, however, the head and neck of the cock become a beautiful golden yellow, as does the breast, and the chin turns almost black. In this plumage the cock baya is very easily recognised.

This species occurs in all parts of India except Bengal, Assam, and Burma. In these places it is replaced by an allied species (71). (Illus. F. II., p. 173; also B. B., p. 131.)

71. *Ploceus megarhynchus:* The Eastern Baya. (F. 721), (J. 694), (I.)

This species differs so little from (No. 70) *P. baya*, that I am inclined to regard it as a local race of the latter species.

72. *Ploceus bengalensis:* The Black-throated Weaver-bird. (F. 722), (J. 696), (– I.)

This species is very like 70 and 71 in appearance, but may be distinguished by (1) a yellow patch on the side of the neck, (2) the black breast, (3) by the fact that the tubular entrance to the nest is short and not long like that of *P. baya* and *P. megarhynchus*.

This is a comparatively rare species and is not found in S. India.

73. *Ploceus manyar:* The Striated Weaver-bird. (F. 723), (J. 695), (I.)

This species is distinguishable from Nos. 70, 71, and 72, by having the feathers of the breast streaked longitudinally with black.

It is found all over India, but is not nearly so commonly seen as *P. baya*.

The Munias, 74–79

Munias are diminutive birds, considerably smaller than the sparrow, characterised by very thick bills. Except when breeding they usually go about in flocks. The nest, which is rarely situated at any great distance from the ground, is a large, ball-like structure, having an entrance at the side. The eggs are white.

74. *Munia malacca:* The Black-headed Munia. (F. 725), (J. 697), (– I.)

Head and breast black, back wings and tail rich chestnut, tinged with maroon. Abdomen white, rest of lower plumage black. Bill very pale slate colour.

This handsome species is confined to S. India; in the north it is replaced by a closely allied species (75).

75. *Munia atricapilla:* The Chestnut-bellied Munia. (F. 726), (J. 698), (– I.)

This differs from 74 only in having the abdomen chestnut instead of white.

76. *Uroloncha malabarica:* The White-throated Munia (called the *Chiruka* in N. India). (F. 734), (J. 703), (– I.)

Jerdon's name for this bird—the Plain

Brown Munia—is much more appropriate than that given it by Oates, for the white of the throat is rarely, if ever, pure, being usually cream-coloured.

This is the species of munia most commonly seen, and is found in all parts of the plains of India, save Eastern Bengal and Burma.

It is a plainly-coloured bird, the upper plumage being earthy brown save for a white patch on the rump. The lower plumage is dirty white. It has a twittering, sparrow-like note, syllabised by Sykes as "*cheet, cheet, cheet.*" The feathers of the tail are graduated. This, the small size of the bird, the white patch on the rump, the thick bill, and the note should serve to enable the observer to identify this inconspicuous little munia. (Illus. B. B., p. 137.)

77. *Uroloncha punctulata:* The Spotted Munia. (F. 735), (J. 699), (– I.)

This is known by bird fanciers as the Nutmeg Bird and the Spice Bird. It, like No. 79, is one of the common cage birds of India.

Head, neck, upper plumage, wings, and tail are rich chocolate brown, that of the head being darkest. The lower breast and abdomen are white, but most of the feathers have each a narrow black semicircular bar, so that the lower parts of the bird have the appearance of a nutmeg-grater: hence one of the popular names of the bird. Bill dark slaty blue.

Does not occur in N.W. F. P. or Sind. (Illus. G. B., p. 16.)

78. *Stictospiza formosa:* The Green Munia, or Green Waxbill. (F. 737), (J. 705), (– I.)

This beautiful little bird, which is barely two-thirds the size of the sparrow, is frequently caged. The upper plumage and wings are light green, brighter in the cock than in the hen; the tail is black, the lower parts are yellow, brighter in the cock than in the hen. Bill bright red.

Distribution: Central India and Southern Bengal.

79. *Sporæginthus amandava:* The Indian Red Munia, or Red Waxbill, or Lal, or Amadavat. (F. 738), (J. 704), (– I.)

Every aviary in India boasts one or two amadavats.

This is a tiny little bird with a bright red beak and red eyes. The general hue of the plumage is reddish brown with patches of the richest crimson and some tiny white spots. There is more crimson in the cock than in the hen, and in the former in the breeding season than at other times of the year. But in both sexes there is always a patch of crimson on the lower rump. In full dress the cock has the whole head, upper plumage, breast, and sides of the body crimson. As, however, the wing feathers are brown, the little birds look brown, and not crimson, during flight. In order to perceive the crimson they must be watched when at rest in the sunlight.

They are highly gregarious and are found all over India. In Burma this bird is replaced by an allied one (*S. flavidiventris*), having the abdomen yellowish red instead of black. (Illus. G. B., frontispiece.)

The Finches, 80–82

These are seed-eating birds, characterised by a thick, stout bill. The canary and the house sparrow are the most familiar examples of this family.

80. *Carpodacus erythninus:* The Common Rose-Finch. (F. 761), (J. 738), (+I.)

Cock: A crimson bird, with brownish-green wings. The crimson is bright on the breast, throat, and rump. There are two yellowish-brown bars on the wing.

Hen: A greenish-brown sparrow-like bird with two conspicuous whitish bars on the wing.

This bird is a winter visitor to the plains of Northern and Central India, and, to some extent, S. India. Natives call it the *Tuti*. It has a pleasing song, but is not a bird that obtrudes itself on the observer. Unless carefully watched for it is apt to be overlooked.

Jerdon writes of this species, " It visits the plains during October, and leaves in April. In March many are taken in fine breeding livery. In the extreme south I have chiefly seen it in bamboo jungle, feeding on the seeds of bamboos on several occasions, and so much is this its habit that the Telegu name signifies 'Bamboo sparrow.' In other parts of the country it frequents alike groves, gardens, and jungle, feeding on various seeds and grain; also not infrequently on flower buds and young leaves."

Eha does not include this species in his *Common Birds of Bombay*. Cunningham says it is fairly common in the gardens of Calcutta during the winter months. Jesse states that it is fairly common at Lucknow. At Lahore I observed it only in March and April.

81. *Gymnorhis flavicollis:* The Yellow-throated Sparrow. (F. 775), (J. 711), (I.)

A near relative of the common house sparrow. In appearance it is like a particularly tidy and slenderly built hen sparrow. It may be readily distinguished by its having a pale yellow patch on the throat, bright in the cock and dull in the hen.

This species frequents gardens, but is far less familiar in its behaviour than *Passer domesticus.* It nests in holes, usually in trees.

Not found so far east as Calcutta. In the Punjab it is a summer visitor, whither it repairs for breeding purposes.

82. *Passer domesticus:* The Common Sparrow or House Sparrow. (F. 776), (J. 706), (I.)

Description of this familiar and ubiquitous bird is quite superfluous. I give it merely for the sake of completeness.

Cock: Top of head and lower back ashy grey, throat black, cheeks and sides of neck pure white, streak over the eye and upper back chestnut, wings and tail brown, the former with a white bar; lower plumage dirty white.

Hen: A dull brown bird with dirty white under parts; reddish-white eyebrow and white wing bar.

The Buntings, 83–85

The yellow-hammer, with its song of "A little bit of bread and *no* che-e-e-ese," has rendered the bunting clan familiar to every Englishman. Buntings are finch-like birds with conical bills, mostly rather larger than the sparrow.

Several species visit the plains of India in large numbers every cold weather and wax fat on the grain crops. They occur in large noisy flocks, making merry among the various cereal crops and taking refuge in trees when disturbed. The species most commonly seen are *E. buchanani*, *E. melanocephala*, and *E. luteola*.

83. *Emberiza buchanani:* The Grey-necked Bunting. (F. 795), (J. 716), (+I.)

There is nothing striking in the appearance of this bird. The upper plumage is ashy brown, the shaft of each feather being darker than the web, giving the bird a streaked appearance. The lower parts are reddish brown. There is some white in the tail visible only during flight. There is an inconspicuous white ring round the eye.

This occurs only in the N.W. parts of India.

84. *Emberiza melanocephala:* The Black-headed Bunting. (F. 799), (J. 721), (+I.)

Cock: The feathers of the head are black with a grey border, so that the head looks grey when the bird first reaches India in the autumn, but gets blacker as the grey edges of the feathers become worn away. The back and shoulders are rich chestnut, the wings and tail are brown, the cheeks and lower plumage are deep bright yellow.

Hen: A brownish bird with dull yellow breast and abdomen and a bright yellow patch under the tail. This species looks rather like a large long-tailed weaver-bird.

Found in winter, and only in N.W. F. P., Punjab, C. P., and Bombay. It is the species of bunting most abundant in the neighbourhood of Bombay, where, as Eha says, it "about takes the place in India of the yellow-hammer at home, swarming about fields and hedges and singing with more cheer than music." (Illus. B. B., p. 142.)

85. *Emberiza luteola:* The Red-headed Bunting. (F. 800), (J. 722), (+I.)

A greenish-brown bird, with the head in the cock a colour between that of chestnut and old gold. Rump yellow, lower plumage yellow, bright in male and duller in female.

Winter visitor to N.W. and Central India.

N.B.—None of the above buntings occur in Madras.

The Swallows, 86–90

Swallows and martins form a well-marked and familiar group of birds. The only other family with which it is possible to confound them is that of the swifts. Anatomically the two families are far removed from one another; but similarity of profession has brought about similarity in outward appearance. Nevertheless, the representatives of the two families may be distinguished at a glance as they dash through the air. "As a swallow darts along," writes Eha, "its wings almost close against its sides at every stroke, and it looks like a pair of scissors opening and shutting. Now a swift never closes its wings in this way. It whips the air rapidly with the points of them, but they are always extended and evenly curved from tip to tip, like a bow, the slim body of the bird being the arrow." Jefferies likens a flying swift to an anchor with enormous flukes. Another difference between the swifts and the swallows is that the former never perch on trees or wires or on the ground, while the latter habitually seat themselves on branches of trees and telegraph wires.

A small bird that dashes with great speed through the air, frequently changing its course, flying now high up, now just skimming the ground, and seeming never to tire, can be nothing other than a swift or a swallow. By the tests given above it is easy to determine whether any particular bird is a swift or a swallow, but having got thus far it is a matter of greater difficulty to determine the species. (Illus. F. II., p. 267; also B. B., p. 35.)

Twenty-two species of swallow are found in India; of these the following are most commonly seen:

86. *Cotile sinensis*: The Indian Sand-martin. (F. 809), (J. 88), (– I.)

A tiny swallow, only about two-thirds the size of the sparrow. Upper plumage greyish brown. Chin and breast greyish white, rest of lower plumage white.

It nests in sandbanks, frequently in company. Occurs only in N. India.

87. *Ptyonoprogne concolor*: The Dusky Crag-martin. (F. 811), (J. 90), (– I.)

Upper plumage dark brown. Some white

spots on the tail. Lower plumage dark brown, paler on the breast. The most dull-coloured of the swallows. It builds a nest like that of the common martin—a saucer of mud stuck on to some vertical surface, usually a cliff or the wall of a cave.

88. *Hirundo rustica :* The Common Swallow (F. 813), (J. 82), (I, but with a deeply forked tail 4½ inches in length.)

Upper plumage glossy steel blue, wings and tail black ; some white in tail. Lower plumage reddish yellow ; forehead, chin, and throat chestnut red.

89. *Hirundo smithii :* The Wire-tailed Swallow. (F. 818), (J. 84), (– I, with the two outer feathers of the tail, the ends of which look like wires, 7 inches in length.)

Head chestnut, upper plumage glossy steel blue, lower plumage pure white.

Not found in Madras or east of the U. P. Builds cup-shaped nest of mud, usually under a bridge or culvert ; sometimes in a verandah. Eggs white with small red splashes.

90. *Hirundo erythropygia :* Sykes's Striated Swallow, or the Red-rumped Swallow. (F. 823), (J. 85), (– I, with a forked tail over 3 inches in length.)

Upper parts glossy steel blue, except for the sides of the head and the lower back, which are chestnut red. Lower plumage pale reddish yellow.

Not found in Madras, Eastern Bengal, or Burma. Nest of usual swallow type; eggs white.

Key to the Common Swallows

A.—*Tail short.*

- *a.* Under parts light—*Cotile sinensis.*
- *b.* Under parts dark—*Ptyonoprogne concolor.*

B.—*Tail long and forked.*

- *a.* Chestnut red on forehead, chin, and throat—*Hirundo rustica.*
- *b.* Head only chestnut, under parts white, outer tail feathers very long and wire-like—*H. smithii.*
- *c.* Chestnut on lower back—*H. erythropygia.*

The Wagtails, 91–94

This family includes the wagtails and pipits. These are slenderly built birds, whose line of flight is an undulating curve. They feed on the ground, sometimes making little sallies into the air after their quarry, and run with great speed. They never hop. They constantly "wag the tail," hence their popular name. The wagtails are distinguished from the pipits by their brighter colouring and longer tails. Pipits are earth-coloured birds with dark stripes along the vein of each feather.

All the wagtails except *M. maderaspatensis* are merely winter visitors to the plains of India.

91. *Motacilla alba:* The White Wagtail. (F. 826), (J. 591), (– II.)

General colour of plumage grey. Face, chin, and throat white, back of head and nape black; a black patch on the breast, the remainder of the lower plumage is white. The wings are black with much white in them. The middle tail feathers are black, the outer ones white. [In all wagtails the outer tail feathers are white, and show up very distinctly during flight.]

Not found in S. India. (Illus. B. B., p. 111.)

92. *Motacilla maderaspatensis:* The Large Pied Wagtail. (F. 831), (J. 589), (II.)

A black bird with a conspicuous white eyebrow. The breast and lower plumage are white. There is a broad white bar in the wing. The outer tail feathers are white.

The only bird with which this wagtail can possibly be confounded is the cock magpie-robin, or *Dhayal* (68) (q.v.), but the two are easily distinguishable by—

(1) The magpie-robin lacks the white eyebrows.

(2) The magpie-robin carries his tail erect; the wagtail never erects its tail.

Not found in Eastern Bengal, Assam, or Burma. A permanent resident. Nests in a hole in an old boat, a roof, a bridge, etc. The eggs are greenish white, blotched with brown.

This wagtail is a fine songster, and may sometimes be seen sitting on a telegraph wire pouring forth its melody. (Illus. B. D., p. 14.)

93. *Motacilla melanope:* The Grey Wagtail. (F. 832), (J. 592), (– II.)

This bird is misnamed. It has a large amount of yellow in its plumage. For this reason Jerdon calls it the grey and yellow wagtail.

The upper parts are bluish grey, marked with yellowish green on the lower back. Throat white, lower plumage bright yellow, wings brown, middle tail feathers black, outer ones white.

94. *Motacilla borealis:* The Grey-headed Wagtail. (F. 833), (J. 593), (– II.)

This species is so like *M. melanope* (No. 93) that it is not easy to differentiate between them. It is, however, generally possible to distinguish them by the fact that in this species the chin is yellow, and the breast is sometimes mottled with black.

The Pipits, 95 *and* 96

95. *Anthus maculatus:* The Indian Tree-Pipit. (F. 841), (J. 596), (I.)

A dull-coloured bird like a wagtail in shape, but with a shorter tail, which it sometimes wags in a half-hearted manner.

The upper parts are earthy brown with dark streaks. The lower parts are creamy white with black streaks. There is a little white in the tail, visible only during flight. It feeds on the ground, but takes refuge in a tree when disturbed. It frequently goes about in flocks. There is nothing striking in its appearance or habits, and so it is not easy to describe satisfactorily.

A winter visitor. Not found in Madras. (Illus. B. B., p. 111).

96. *Anthus rufulus:* The Indian Pipit, or the Indian Tit-Lark. (F. 847), (J. 600), (I.)

This is scarcely distinguishable from the last species (95). It has a somewhat longer bill and longer legs. The claw of its hind toe is much longer than that of *A. maculatus*, but this cannot be seen unless the bird be held in the hand. This species is found all over India. Thus in N. India in winter a bird answering to this description may be either species, and it is only safe to set it down as a "pipit."

The Larks, 97–103

Larks are so like pipits that it is not easy to distinguish between them without capturing them. (Illus. F. II., p. 315.)

97. *Alauda gulgula:* The Indian Skylark. (F. 861), (J. 767), (+I.)

This is very like the above two pipits in appearance, but there is a good deal more white in the tail. Except for its somewhat smaller size it is indistinguishable from the English skylark, and all books on Indian ornithology state that this bird soars up into the heavens and pours forth its song just as the lark does in England. I must confess that this is not my experience. I have never seen this species soar in the middle of the day, or at any time save the very early morning.

This is a permanent resident and builds a nest on the ground like that of the common skylark.

98. *Alaudula raytal:* The Ganges Sand-lark. (F. 866), (J. 762), (–I.)

This is distinguishable from the skylark by its smaller size and its white under plumage.

It is a permanent resident, but is confined to the sandy beds of the rivers of N. India. It runs about near the edge of the water.

The Bush Larks, 99 *and* 100

These are distinguished by having no white in the tail. They frequently perch in bushes or low trees, whence they sometimes take short flights in the air.

99. *Mirafra assamica:* The Bengal Bush-lark. (F. 870), (J. 754), (I.)

Found in U. P., Bengal, and Assam.

100. *Mirafra affinis:* The Madras Bush-lark. (F. 872), (J. 755), (I.)

Found in S. India. It is common in Guindy Park.

The Crested Larks, 101–103

These are readily distinguished by the sharp-pointed crest which projects backwards and upwards from the back of the head. They sing well and have habits very similar to those of the skylark. No white in the tail.

101. *Galerita cristata:* The Crested Lark. (F. 874), (J. 769), (+I.)

Punjab and U. P., where it is abundant. Very common at Lahore.

102. *Galerita deva:* Sykes's Crested Lark. (F. 875), (J. 765), (I.).

U. P., Rajputana, and C. I.

103. *Galerita malabarica:* The Malabar Crested Lark. (F. 876), (J. 768), (+I.)

Bombay and Travancore.

The Finch-Larks, 104 *and* 105

These are easily recognised by their curious habit of flying some twenty or thirty feet into the air, then closing their wings and dropping to the ground. As they descend they utter a curious note. They are dumpy little birds and do not look as large as their measurements.

104. *Ammomanes phœnicura:* The Rufous-tailed Finch-Lark. (F. 877), (J. 758), (I.)

A dark brown bird, with dark red on the lower back and tail.

It is found chiefly in Central India in Bombay. In Sind and the Punjab it is replaced by *A. phœnicuroides* (the Desert Finch-Lark). Not found in Madras.

105. *Pyrrhulauda grisea:* The Ashy-crowned Finch-Lark. (F. 879), (J. 760), (– I.)

This is the common Finch-Lark of India, being a permanent resident everywhere, except the N.W. F. P., Eastern Bengal, Assam, and Burma.

Cock: Upper parts dark ashy grey. Streak through the eye and all the lower plumage black, cheeks and sides of breast white, so that, as Eha points out, the black on the throat takes the form of a cross. [This very unusual colouring, i.e. darker below than above, renders the cock easy to identify.]

Hen: The parts that are black in the cock are reddish brown. (Illus. B. B., p. 142.)

The Sunbirds, or Honeysuckers, 106–108

These charming little birds are easy to identify. They are the Old World counterparts of the humming birds of the New World. The hens are inconspicuous little brown birds with yellow under parts, but the cocks wear a gay livery. They build large hanging nests, composed of dried grass, leaves, etc., held together by cobweb, so that they look, from a little distance, like hanging masses of rubbish. Close inspection shows that the nest is pear-shaped, with a circular entrance at one side and a little porch over the entrance. The nests are found in gardens, being sometimes suspended from the roof of the verandah.

These birds feed largely on the nectar of flowers, which they abstract by means of their long tubular tongues. In order to obtain the honey they frequently hover on rapidly-vibrating wings, like humming birds.

106. *Arachnechthra lotenia:* Loten's Sunbird. (F. 894), (J. 235), (– I.)

Cock: The whole plumage is dark metallic purple, looking black in some lights, but in the sun's rays it displays a green or lilac sheen. The beak is long and curved.

Hen: Upper plumage earthy brown, lower plumage very pale yellow.

Found only in S. India. Very common in Madras. (Illus. B. P., pp. 78, 82, and 90.)

107. *Arachnechthra asiatica:* The Purple Sunbird. (F. 895), (J. 234), (– I.)

Cock : Very like *A. lotenia*, but this species is smaller and its curved beak is shorter. It is a very fine songster, its voice being as sweet as that of the canary or the pied wagtail.

Hen : Upper plumage earthy brown, lower plumage yellow.

Found all over India, but is only a summer visitor to the Punjab and N.W. F. P. (Illus. I. F., frontispiece.)

108. *Arachnechthra zeylonica :* The Purple-rumped Sunbird (F. 901), (J. 232), (– I.)

Cock : From a little distance the cock looks like a black-and-white bird, the upper parts and breast appear black, and the lower parts white. Closer inspection, however, reveals a livery of many colours, each of which has a beautiful sheen. There is a patch on the crown which appears metallic lilac in some lights and emerald green in others. The neck and upper back are dull crimson, the lower back, chin, and throat are brilliant metallic purple. The tail and wing feathers are dark brown. There is a maroon collar below the throat. The lower plumage is bright yellow.

Hen : Upper plumage earthy brown, lower parts yellow.

Found in all parts of India except N.W. F. P.,

Punjab, Assam, and Burma. Very common in S. India. (Illus. B. P., p. 80; also B. B., p. 62, and G. B., p. 40, and I. F., p. 128.)

The Pittas, 109

Pittas are unique birds. They are about the size of a quail and are characterised by their short tails and legs and their many-coloured plumage. They feed upon the ground, but when alarmed they take refuge in bushes. They are never seen far from cover. They have a cheery whistling song.

109. *Pitta brachyura:* The Indian Pitta. (F. 933), (J. 345), (II.)

The natives call this species the *Naurang* (nine colours) on account of its many colours.

The crown is yellow tinged with orange and divided in the middle by a broad black band running from the beak to the nape of the neck, where it meets a broader black band that passes below the eye. The eyebrow is white. The back and shoulders are dull bluish green. There is a patch of pale blue feathers over the tail and a patch of the same colour on the wing. The feathers of the wing and tail are black tipped with blue. There is a white bar in the wing visible only during flight. Chin and throat are white, breast orange-yellow. There is a large crimson patch under the tail.

Not found in N.W. F. P., Punjab, Eastern Bengal, Assam, or Burma. It is nowhere abundant, but fairly common in Madras. (Illus. B. D., p. 108 ; also I. F., p. 256.)

The Woodpeckers, 110 *and* 111

A general description of the woodpeckers is scarcely necessary. They feed exclusively on insects, which they pick off the trunks of trees, tapping the same with their chisel-like beak to drive their quarry from its lair. They are very skilled climbers, moving up and down the tree trunk in a series of jerks ; the head is always pointing upwards. Their powers of flight are not great, they progress through the air in a series of undulations, uttering their peculiar harsh cries. They excavate their nests in the trunks of trees. A great many woodpeckers exist in India, but only two species are widely distributed.

110. *Liopicus mahrattensis*: The Yellow-fronted Pied Woodpecker. (F. 972), (J. 160), (+I.)

A spotted black-and-white bird, with a yellow patch on the forehead. The cock has in addition a short red crest. There is also a patch of red on the abdomen.

Not found in Eastern Bengal and Assam.

111. *Brachypternus aurantius:* The Golden-backed Woodpecker. (F. 986), (J. 180), (+III.)

Bright crimson crest. Top of head black. Sides of head white, with a number of black lines and streaks. Upper back golden yellow. Lower back and tail black. Wings black and golden yellow, with some white spots. It has a loud screaming call, which it constantly utters.

Not found in Assam. Common in all other parts of India. (Illus. F. III., p. 14; also B. C., p. 65.)

112. *Iynx torquilla:* The Common Wryneck. (F. 1003), J. 188), (+I.)

An inconspicuous grey - brownish bird, streaked, speckled, and mottled all over its plumage. In some respects its habits are those of the woodpecker, but it rarely if ever climbs high up a tree, it is usually seen picking insects off a tree stump or a mound. It has a peculiar habit of twisting its head round, hence its name.

It is a winter visitor to the plains of India, but can scarcely be called a common bird.

The Barbets, 113 *and* 114

Barbets are tree-haunting birds with thick bills. They have loud monotonous calls of two or three notes, which they repeat eternally. They nest in holes in trees, which they excavate with their thick stout bills, in woodpecker fashion. The entrance to the nest is a perfectly circular hole, like that leading to a woodpecker's nest, but considerably smaller. Barbets, when calling, move the head, so that it is not easy to locate the bird from its call.

113. *Thereiceryx zeylonicus:* The Common Green Barbet. (F. 1008), (J. 193), (III.)

A rich leaf-green bird, with a brownish head and a large brown patch round the eye devoid of feathers.

During the latter part of the cold weather and the early part of the hot weather it makes the *bagh* where it occurs resound with its loud, penetrating, monotonous *kutur*, *kutur*, *kutur*. The bird starts by uttering a harsh laugh—*tur-r-r-r*—this is followed by a long succession of *kuturs*.

Not found in Punjab, Sind, Rajputana, Lower Bengal, or the East Coast of the Madras presidency.

114. *Xantholæma hæmatocephala:* The Crimson-breasted Barbet, or Coppersmith. (F. 1019), (J. 197), (+I.)

An olive-green bird with very gaudy colouring on the head. I quote the following description from *Bombay Ducks:* The bird "always puts me in mind of a woman who 'makes up' very carelessly, who is not only exceedingly lavish of the paint, but does not understand how to shade it off gradually. The general colour of the bird's plumage is greenish, but on close inspection many greyish white feathers are seen to be mingled with the green ones. There is a daub of crimson on the forehead and another on the throat. The sides of the face are pale yellow. The legs are coral red. The build of the bird is exceedingly coarse."

But the coppersmith is a bird that is usually heard rather than seen. Its monotonous metallic *tonk*, *tonk*, *tonk*, like the tapping of a hammer on metal, is one of the most familiar sounds of the Indian country-side. This cry is heard only in the hot weather, and the warmer the day the more vigorously does the bird call. (Illus. B. D., p. 246; also B. B., p. 57.)

115. *Coracias indica:* The Indian Roller, or "Blue Jay." (F. 1022), (J. 123), (+III.)

This is a most familiar bird. Its head and neck, throat and shoulders, are the colour of a faded port-wine stain. Its wings and tail are composed of alternate broad bands of light and dark blue. These organs are not very much *en evidence* when the bird is perched; but flight transforms it; as it flaps heavily along it is a study in Oxford and Cambridge blue.

It is found in most parts of India, but not in the island of Bombay.

It nests at the beginning of the hot weather in a hole in a building or a decayed tree. At the breeding season it is very noisy, uttering strange hoarse cries as it performs weird antics in the air, or, sitting on a perch, it every now and again utters a loud *tshock*, accompanied by a vibration of the tail.

In Burma this species is replaced by an allied one—*Coracias affinis*—the Burmese Roller. (Illus. B. D., p. 112; also B. P., p. 12, and B. C. cover.)

The Bee-eaters, 116 *and* 117

Bee-eaters are brightly coloured birds of elegant form. They are characterised by having the median pair of tail feathers prolonged a couple of inches beyond the others as bristles. The feeding habits of these birds are like those of flycatchers. They make from some perch little sallies in the air after insects. The wings when spread are triangular in shape. They excavate their nests in sandbanks.

116. *Merops viridis:* The Common Indian Bee-eater. (F. 1026), (J. 117), (I, but with rather a long tail.)

An emerald-green bird with a turquoise throat, black necklace, and a black band through the eye. The wings are shot with bronze, so that, as the bird sails along on outstretched pinions, it looks now green, now bronze, as the rays of the sun are reflected at different angles. There is some black in the tail, and the two median tail feathers project as bristles a couple of inches beyond the other tail feathers. The eye is bright red.

Found all over India, but undergoes a considerable amount of local migration. It is a summer visitor to the Punjab and N.W. F. P., and is said to leave the island of Bombay in the hot weather. (Illus. B. D., p. 82; also B. B., p. 42, and G. B., p. 64.)

117. *Merops philippinus:* The Blue-tailed Bee-eater. (F. 1027), (J. 118), (II, but with rather a long tail.)

General hue green, shot with bronze; the tail is bluish. There is a broad black streak running through the eye. The chin is a dirty cream colour. The throat is chestnut-red. The eye is bright red.

This species is a larger and less beautiful edition of No. 116. Like the latter it undergoes partial migration, being a summer visitor to N. India and a winter visitor to S. India. One sees large numbers of these birds when out snipe shooting in Madras. They perch on the *bands* between the flooded fields and make sallies into the air after insects. The note is a feeble but mellow whistle.

The Kingfishers, 118–120

These form a very well-marked group of piscatorial birds, characterised by long bills and short tails. They nest in holes in river banks.

118. *Ceryle varia:* The Indian Pied Kingfisher. (F. 1033), (J. 136), (III.)

This bird must be familiar to every Anglo-Indian, it is the "Pied Fish-tiger" of Sir Edwin Arnold. It is speckled black and white like a Hamburgh fowl. It seeks its quarry by hanging in the air on rapidly vibrating wings high above the water. Suddenly its pinions cease quivering, and it drops like a stone into the water. Sometimes it checks its fall before reaching the water, and flies to another part of the *jhil*, where it again hovers.

It is impossible to mistake this bird; there is no other like it save its larger Himalayan brother (*C. lugubris*). It has a small crest. (Illus. B. D., p. 66; also I. F., p. 162.)

119. *Alcedo ispida:* The Common Kingfisher. (F. 1035), (J. 134), (II, but with a very short tail.)

This bird, which is to be found in all parts of India where there is a river, a tank, or a pool of water, is the kingfisher with which we are familiar in England.

Its head and nape are blue with faint black cross bars. The back is bright pale blue; the tail is dark blue; the wings greenish blue. The sides of the head are studies in red, blue, black, and white. The chin is whitish or cream-coloured, and the lower parts are rusty red. The bill is black; the feet are coral-red.

Its habit is to perch on a bough overhanging the water, or on the river bank itself, and thence to dive obliquely into the water after its quarry. Its flight is low, straight, and very rapid; when in motion it continually utters a peculiar whistling scream. Its neck is very short, and as it sits waiting for its quarry it keeps raising and lowering its head in the most comical manner. (Illus. B. D., p. 102; also B. P., p. 144.)

120. *Halcyon smyrnensis:* The White-breasted Kingfisher. (F. 1044), (J. 129), (III.)

This beautiful bird must be familiar to every Anglo-Indian.

The head and nape are rich chocolate brown, as is the abdomen. The back, tail, and wings are bright blue. During flight the wings display a very conspicuous white band. The chin, throat, and breast are white. The bill is dark red, and the feet bright red. It is impossible to mistake this bird; a rapidly flying, bright blue bird, with white wing bars, which emits a loud scream, is without doubt this species.

It is often found far from water, since it feeds largely on insects, which it picks off the ground in much the same way as the roller or so-called blue jay does.

The above three kingfishers are among the commonest birds of India. There are several other species of more restricted distribution; but as these are only common locally, I have not included them in this work. The reader should experience no difficulty in identifying them with the aid of the descriptions in the *Fauna of British India*. (Illus. B. D., p. 104; also B. P., p. 4.)

The Hornbills, 121 *and* 122

These include some of the strangest forms in nature. They are often erroneously called Toucans by Anglo-Indians. Toucans do not occur in India. Hornbills are characterised by the enormous development of the bill. I have elsewhere described the largest of the hornbills as follows: *Dichoceros bicornis* is "nearly 4½ feet in length. The body is only 14 inches long, being an insignificant part of the bird, a mere connecting link between the massive beak and the great loosely inserted tail. The beak is nearly a foot in length, and is rendered more conspicuous than it would otherwise be by a structure known as a casque. This is a horny excrescence nearly as large as the bill, which causes the bird to look as though it were wearing a hat, which it had placed for a joke on its beak rather than its head. The eye is red, and the upper lid is fringed with eyelashes which add still further to the oddity of the bird's appearance."

The nesting habits of these birds are curious. They nestle in holes in trees. When the eggs are laid the hen goes into the hole, the entrance to which is plastered up by the cock and hen until the orifice is only just large enough to allow of the insertion of the beak. Thus the hen remains a voluntary prisoner until the young are ready to leave the nest, the cock bringing food to her.

The great majority of hornbills are confined to the large forests, and so cannot be called common birds. Two of the smaller species, however, are more widely distributed. (Illus. F. III., p. 140.)

121. *Lophoceros birostris:* The Common Grey Hornbill. (F. 1062), (J. 144), (IV, but with the tail a foot long.)

A large brownish-grey bird, darkest on the sides of the head and palest on the lower parts. The bill, which has a small casque or excrescence on top, is blackish and 4 inches long. It is a tree-haunting species. Its cry is very characteristic. Its flight is laboured, consisting of " alternate flappings and sailings," like that of the tree-pie.

This species is common in Oudh. Blanford states that it is wanting in the Punjab. This is not correct, as I have seen it in Lahore. I have not observed it in the vicinity of Madras. Eha does not mention it in his common *Birds of Bombay*, nor does it appear to be found in the neighbourhood of Calcutta.

122. *Lophoceros griseus :* The Malabar Grey Hornbill. (F. 1063), (J. 145), (IV, but with tail 9 inches long.)

This is very like 121, but it lacks the casque. It is the common hornbill of the West Coast.

The Hoopoes, 123

Hoopoes are ground-feeding birds, characterised by their long slightly curved bill and conspicuous crest, which ordinarily projects from the back of the head and looks like a backward continuation of the beak. When the bird is disturbed and when it flies the crest is expanded like a fan. Almost every lawn in India forms the feeding-ground for at least one pair of hoopoes. Hoopoes nest in holes in trees or in the walls of buildings.

123. *Upupa indica:* The Indian Hoopoe. (F. 1067), (J. 255), (III.)

Head and body fawn-coloured. Wings and tail white with very broad black bars. The beak is 2½ inches long, and the legs are very short. The feathers of the crest have black tips. The note is a soft *ūk—ūk—ūk*, rapidly repeated. (Illus. B. D., p. 140.)

The Swifts, 124 *and* 125

These birds are frequently confounded with swallows (q.v.). Many species visit India, but only two are really common birds.

124. *Cypselus affinis:* The Common Indian Swift. (F. 1073), (J. 100), (–I.)

A blackish bird, with a white bar across the back, which flies with great velocity; the wings form the arc of a circle as it dashes through the air. It never perches. When it wishes to rest it repairs to its nest, which is a saucer-shaped structure made of mud, bits of straw, feathers, etc., usually fixed on to a wall under an eave, sometimes in a deserted temple or mosque. (Illus. B. B., p. 35.)

125. *Tachornis batassiensis:* The Palm-swift. (F. 1075), (J. 102), (–I.)

A brownish-black bird. Its habits are like those of No. 124, except that its flight is less swift and it is rarely found away from palm trees. It attaches its nest to the under side of a palm leaf, or a betel-nut leaf.

The Nightjars, 126 *and* 127

These birds are very nocturnal in their habits, so, like the heroine of *The Diary of a Bad Girl,* they are heard and not seen.

They are characterised by the large mouth, which enables them to secure their insect quarry while they are on the wing. They usually lie up during the day on the ground in some secluded spot.

126. *Caprimulgus asiaticus:* The Common Indian Nightjar, or Goatsucker. (F. 1091), (J. 112), (+II.)

Upper parts greyish brown, lower parts reddish brown, every feather being marked by a number of narrow blackish cross bars.

The voice of this bird must be familiar to many residents in India, it sounds like a stone skimming over ice, and hence is known as the ice-bird.

127. *Caprimulgus macrurus:* Horsfield's Nightjar. (F. 1093), (J. 110), (+III.)

A large edition of No. 126. Its *chuk*, *chuk*, *chuk* is not unlike the sound made by tapping a plank with a hammer.

The Cuckoos, 128–131

This large family falls into two classes—the parasitic and the non-parasitic—both classes being represented in India.

The European cuckoo is very abundant in the Himalayas, but is rarely seen or heard in the plains.

128. *Hierococcyx varius:* The Common Hawk-Cuckoo—the Brain-fever bird of Anglo-Indians. (F. 1109), (J. 205), (– III, but with a tail 6 inches long.)

Every Anglo-Indian is familiar with the *crescendo* shriek—brain-fever, ***brain-fever***, BRAIN-FEVER—of this bird, which is reiterated with such "damnable persistency" at the beginning of the hot weather. This bird is exceedingly common in the United Provinces. It is less abundant in other parts of India. It does not appear to occur west of Umballa; I never heard it in Madras, and it does not seem to occur in the island of Bombay. It is impossible to miss it where it does occur. There is no mistaking its note. It is a greyish-brown bird with whitish under parts, each feather having darker cross bars. The bird is very hawk-like in appearance, hence its name.

It is parasitic on "The Seven Sisters" and other kinds of babblers. (Illus. B. C., p. 95.)

129. *Coccystes jacobinus:* The Pied-crested Cuckoo. Known to Europeans in Upper India as the Rainy-weather Bird. (F. 1118), (J. 212), (+II, but with a tail over 6 inches long.)

Upper plumage glossy black, with a broad white wing-bar, and white tips to the tail feathers. The chin, throat, and under parts are white. A conspicuous black crest.

This species is very common "on the Bombay side." Numbers visit Northern India in the rains, and announce their presence by loud high-pitched cries.

It is parasitic on various species of babblers. (Illus. B. B., p. 53.)

130. *Eudynamis honorata:* The Indian Koel,

sometimes wrongly called (e.g. in *The Common Birds of Bombay*) the Brain-fever Bird. (F. 1120), (J. 214), (III, but with a tail 8 inches long.)

Cock: A glossy black bird with a green bill and crimson eye. As he flies he looks like a slenderly built crow with an unusually long tail.

Hen: A brown bird, spotted and barred all over with white. Bill and eye as in cock. This is an exceedingly noisy bird, and is most vociferous at dawn. It has three distinct calls. The commonest is a *crescendo:* ku-il, ***ku-il***, KU-IL, whence its name. Another call is ***ku-y-o***. The third is a torrent of ***kekaree***, ***kekarees***. (Illus. B. D., pp. 218 and 220; also B. C., p. 92.)

It is parasitic on crows.

131. *Centropus sinensis:* The Common Coucal, or Crow-Pheasant. (F. 1130), (J. 217), (– IV, but with a tail 10 inches long.)

A great black fowl with chestnut-red wings. It feeds largely on the ground, and its long tail sometimes causes the "griff" to mistake it for a pheasant.

Its call, which is heard at all times of the day, but more especially at dawn, is a low, loud, sonorous *whoot, whoot, whoot,* the kind of call that one associates with an owl.

It is not parasitic, but builds a large domed nest in the innermost recesses of a dense thicket. (Illus. I.F., p. 80. [Illustration not a good one.])

The Green Parrots, 132–134

Every dweller in India must be familiar with these noisy birds, both in the captive and the wild state. They go about in small flocks, looking like "live emeralds in the sun," and uttering loud screams and harsh cries. During flight they turn from side to side "like badly balanced arrows." They nestle in holes in trees or buildings.

Three species are to be numbered among the common birds of India.

132. *Palæornis nepalensis:* The Alexandrine or Large Indian Paroquet. (F. 1135), (J. 147), (+III, but with a tail over a foot long.)

A beautiful grass-green bird, with some blue in the tail and a red patch on each shoulder. The cock has a rose-coloured collar round the back of his neck, which is connected with the bill on each side by a black stripe.

Found in N. and C. India. Very common in the Punjab.

133. *Palæornis torquatus:* The Rose-ringed Paroquet. (F. 1138), (J. 148), (– III, but with a tail 10 inches long.)

A small edition of No. 132, but lacks the red patch on the shoulders.

The commonest of the green parrots, and found all over the plains of India. (Illus. B. P., p. 18; also I. F., p. 220.)

134. *Palæornis cyanocephalus:* The Western Blossom-headed Paroquet. (F. 1139), (J. 149), (II, but with a tail over 8 inches long.)

Cock: General colour bright grass-green. The head is red, tinged with blue, as Blanford says, like the bloom on a plum. There is a red patch on the shoulders, as in the case of No. 132. The median tail feathers are pale blue.

Hen: Differs from the cock in that the head is duller, being of a grey rather than a red hue.

Not found in N.W. F. P. or the Punjab. Commoner in South than in North India.

The Owls, 135–139

Owls form a well-marked natural order It is easy enough to recognise an owl when one sees one, but not easy to say to what species it belongs, because all owls bear a strong resemblance to one another—all are of much the same colour—reddish brown with darker bars or drops. Moreover, they are all creatures of the night, so, save with one exception, are not much *en evidence* in the daytime. This exception is that little clown, the spotted owlet.

135. ***Athene brama:*** The Spotted Owlet. (F. 1180), (J. 76), (II.)

A small owl; upper plumage earthy brown or grey in colour, copiously spotted and barred with white. Lower plumage white with dark brown spots and cross bars.

It comes out long before sunset and pours forth a volley of chuckles and squeaks; two of these individuals often shouting at once. When it catches sight of a human being it stares at him with its bright golden orbs and, as Eha observes, bows with sarcastic effect. No one who has dwelt any length of time in India can fail to have remarked this very noisy little owl. It nests in holes of trees or in the walls of bungalows. This is the only owl which can be classed as a familiar bird. Three other species, however, are often seen, namely (Illus. B. D., p. 256; also B. P., p. 94, and B. B., p. 29):

136. *Strix flammea:* The Barn Owl or Screech Owl. (F. 1152), (J. 60), (IV.)

This is a reddish-brown bird barred with narrow white and black bars. It has a long heart-shaped face, which is white.

It is very nocturnal in its habits; when it does get abroad in the daytime it is promptly mobbed by the crows. Its cry is a weird screech, and it is regarded by the people as a bird of evil omen.

137. *Asio accipitrinus:* The Short-eared Owl. (F. 1157), (J. 68), (+IV.)

A large buff bird barred all over with dark brown. It lies up during the day in grass, and is often flushed by sportsmen. Sometimes three or four are flushed together. It is a winter visitor to India.

138. *Scops giu:* The Scops Owl. (F. 1173), (J. 74), (+I.)

This may be distinguished from the spotted owlet by the fact that it possesses "horns" or ear-tufts. Like most other owls it is heard more often than seen. Its note, which must be familiar to all who have camped in India, is a single hoot, which is repeated monotonously at regular intervals of about ten seconds.

139. *Glaucidium radiatum:* The Jungle Owlet. (F. 1184), (J. 78), (– II.)

This owl is very like 135 in appearance, and has a peculiar protracted call which must be familiar to those who have camped in the U. P.

It does not appear to occur in the N.W. F. P., the Punjab, the Deccan, or Bombay.

140. *Pandion haliaëtus:* The Osprey. (F. 1189), (J. 40), (– V.)

This looks very like a kite when seen as it perches on a stone, but is distinguishable from the kite by the fact that its head and neck are white, save for a broad dark band which runs from the eye down the side of the neck.

When seeking for food, however, nothing is easier than to identify the osprey. Like the pied kingfisher the great bird poises itself in the air on quivering wings high above the water. Suddenly its wings close and it drops down like a falling stone and disappears into the water with a huge splash, to emerge a second or two later with a fish in its talons.

In the cold weather the osprey is to be seen

in most places where there are large *jhils* or backwaters.

The Vultures, 141–145

These are huge birds of prey which feed exclusively on carrion. They are distinguished by the fact that their head and neck are destitute of feathers. A large bird of prey with bare head and neck is undoubtedly a vulture.

Vultures, as everyone knows, stay for hours floating on outstretched wings high up in the air, looking out for dead animals. Kites and other birds of prey remain for long periods on the wing; they, too, can sail and soar, but they do not literally hang in the air as the vultures do. As these latter float in the air it will be observed that their wings project straight out at right angles to the body. The commonest species of vulture are:

141. *Otogyps calvus:* The Black or Pondicherry Vulture. (F. 1191), (J. 2), (+V, nearly twice the size of the kite.)

A black bird with a red head, a white waistcoat, and a white patch on each thigh.

Rare in the Punjab and Sind.

142. *Gyps indicus:* The Indian Long-billed

Vulture. (F. 1194), (J. 4), (+V, over a yard in length.)

Uniform brownish grey; the hue varying with individuals.

Not found in Sind.

143. *Pseudogyps bengalensis:* The Indian White-backed Vulture. (F. 1196), (J. 5), (+V. Between 141 and 142 in size.)

This is the commonest vulture in India. It is very dark grey, almost black. The naked head is rather lighter than the rest of the body. The lower back is white, and this makes the bird easy to identify. It has some white in the wings, and this during flight is visible as a broad white band that runs from the body nearly to the tip of the wing. Thus the wing from below appears to be white with very broad black edges. (Illus. B. B., p. 9.)

144. *Neophron ginginianus:* The Smaller White Scavenger Vulture. (F. 1197), (J. 6), (V.)

This familiar creature I have named "The ugliest bird in the world." I reproduce the description of the bird from *Bombay Ducks:* "There is no other creature like unto it. It is about the size of a kite. Its plumage is dirty white, except the tips of the wings, which are shabby black. The neck is covered with feathers, which stick out like the back hairs of a schoolboy. These are, if possible, rather dirtier-looking than the rest of the plumage, and frequently assume a rusty hue. Its bill is yellow, so are its naked face and its legs. As 'Eha' remarks: 'It does not stand upright like the true vultures, but carries its body like a duck and steps like a recruit.' . . . It is a good flier, and when seen on the wing looks quite a respectable bird. The under parts of its wings appear pure white in the sunlight, and the black border gives them a finish."

Young scavenger vultures are sooty brown when they leave the nest and look like a different species.

This creature feeds on human ordure and haunts the neighbourhood of latrines. It is known to Thomas Atkins as the Shawk. It is also called Pharaoh's Chicken. (Illus. B. D., pp. 278 and 280.)

In the Punjab it is replaced by a species which resembles it in all characters, differing only in being a little larger. This species is:

145. *Neophron percnopterus:* The Egyptian Vulture, or Large White Scavenger Vulture. (F. II., 98), (J. 6), (+V.)

The Birds of Prey, 146–162

This large family is composed of birds which bear so strong a family likeness that it is almost impossible to describe them in such a way as to enable the reader to identify them at sight. As with the owls, birds of prey are easily recognised as such, but to name any particular species baffles even professed ornithologists. To try to make out the raptores by their colour is, to use the words of Eha, "at the best a short road to despair. Naturalists learn to recognise them as David's watchman recognised the courier who brought tidings of the victory over Absalom. 'His running is like the running of Ahimaaz, the son of Zadok.' Every bird of prey has its own character, some trick of flight, something in its figure and proportions which serves to distinguish it decisively." What precisely this something is I am not in most cases able to state. I trust that before long Mr. C. H. Donald, or some other Indian falconer, will give us a little handbook on the birds of prey of this country. For my part I am able merely to attempt a description of two or three of the very commonest forms.

146. *Aquila vindhiana :* The Indian Tawny Eagle. (F. 1203), (J. 29), (+V.)

In colouring this bird is very like the common kite, but has not so long a tail ; and its legs are feathered right down to the toe—this is the sign-manual of all the true eagles. A bird that looks like a kite with feathered legs is probably a tawny eagle—the commonest eagle in India, abundant everywhere save on the Malabar coast.

147. *Butastur teesa :* The White-eyed Buzzard. (F. 1220), (J. 48), (IV.)

This bird of prey is about the size of the common house crow. Eha writes, "A Buzzard's idea of life is to sit upon a pole, or on top of a small tree commanding a good expanse of grass land, and to watch for a field mouse, or a lizard, or even a fat grasshopper. If you see a biggish, untidy hawk, of a sandy brown colour, more or less dashed with whitish, spending the morning in this way, you may put it down as *Butastur teesa.*" The sign-manual of this common bird is its white eye, and if you cannot get near enough to make this out with the aid of field glasses, you may still identify this species by the conspicuous white patch on the nape of the neck.

Very common in N. India; rare in the south.

148. *Haliaëtus leucoryphus:* Pallas's Fishing Eagle. (F. 1223), (J. 42), (+V; nearly half as big again as the kite.)

A large brown bird with whitish forehead, chin, and throat, and a broad white band (4 inches wide) across the tail, about three inches from the tip. This is the sign-manual of this species, and on this account Jerdon calls it "The Ring-tailed Fish Eagle."

Not found in S. India.

"All the fish-eagles," writes C. H. Donald in *The Indian Field*, "have loud resonant calls, anything but melodious, and each and all seem to love hearing their own voices. *H. leucoryphus* in the plains of the Punjab may often be heard long before he is seen, particularly when soaring, and though he himself may only appear a wee speck in the heavens, his call will be distinctly heard."

This bird frequents rivers and marshes, and is an inland rather than a seashore bird.

149. *Haliaëtus leucogaster:* The White-bellied Sea-Eagle. (F. 1224), (J. 43), (V.; a little larger than the kite.)

Head, neck, lower parts, and nearly the

whole of the tail white; other parts dark grey or brown. Jerdon calls this species the Grey-backed Sea-Eagle. This species is very seldom seen inland, and is easily distinguished from Nos. 148 and 150 by having the lower parts white instead of brown.

Col. Cunningham describes this species as "one of the most splendid of large raptorial birds, owing to the brilliant contrast of the snowy whiteness of the head and under surface, with the deep ashy tints of the wings and back. There are few more striking objects than one of them as he sits on a bare branch overhanging a tidal channel, glancing around with his bold black eyes, and with all his beautiful plumage gleaming in the bright sunlight."

This is a very noisy species, especially at the breeding season.

150. *Haliaëtus albicilla:* The White-tailed Sea-Eagle. (F. 1225), (+V; half as big again as a kite.)

A large brown bird with a white tail, of which the middle feathers are considerably longer than the outer ones. By this character and by its loud cries may this bird be identified. It is only a winter visitor to India—to the Punjab, Sind, and the U. P.

151. *Haliastur indus:* The Brahminy Kite. (F. 1228), (J. 55), (– V.)

Of all the birds of prey this is perhaps the easiest to identify in its adult state. The head, neck, breast, and upper abdomen are white, the shaft of each white feather being black. The remainder of the plumage is a rich chestnut, almost maroon.

The young are very like the common kite in appearance, but may be distinguished when on the wing by the fact that the tail of the Brahminy is always rounded, while that of the kite is more or less forked.

This species is rare in the Punjab, common everywhere else. In Madras it sometimes swoops down and carries off a snipe that has been shot by a sportsman. Its cry is a peculiar squeaking wail. (Illus. B. D., p. 190.)

152. *Milvus govinda:* The Common Pariah Kite. (F. 1229), (J. 56), (V.)

Description of this ubiquitous bird is unnecessary. His long tail, slightly forked at the tip, suffices to distinguish him at a glance from all other raptorial birds. (Illus. B. D., p. 182; also B. P., p. 148.)

153. *Circus macrurus:* The Pale Harrier. (F. 1233), (J. 51), (+IV.)

154. *Circus cineraceus:* Montagu's Harrier. (F. 1234), (J. 52), (+IV.)

155. *Circus cyaneus:* The Hen Harrier. (F. 1235), (J. 50), (–V.)

156. *Circus melanoleucus:* The Pied Harrier. (F. 1236), (J. 53), (+IV.)

157. *Circus æruginosus:* The Marsh Harrier. (F. 1237), (J. 54), (–V.)

I shall not attempt to describe these birds, as, although it may be possible to tell the male birds apart, the hens are so alike that to distinguish them is no easy matter. The ordinary man will doubtless be satisfied to call them all harriers.

Harriers are cold-weather visitors to India. They are striking-looking birds with long wings. They fly low, only a few inches above the level of the ground, ever on the look out for a lizard, a mouse, an insect, or even a small bird. They are larger than crows and smaller than kites. They hunt over fields and marshes, and are not seen in towns, but those who shoot must be familiar with them. (Illus. B. B., p. 15.)

158. *Astur badius:* The Shikra. (F.12 44), (J. 23), (+III.)

This is one of the most familiar birds of prey.

It is considerably smaller than the common house crow. Its upper plumage is ashy grey. The tail is of the same hue, but with broad black cross bars. The breast is pale rust colour, with a number of thin wavy white cross bars. The eye is bright yellow, as is the cere or base of the beak. It is very like the Brain-fever Bird in appearance. It often hunts for its quarry in the neighbourhood of trees. Its method is to make a short quick dash. Natives of India very frequently train this bird to hawk quail and mynas. Its note is a sharp double whistle.

159. *Accipiter nisus:* The Sparrow-Hawk. (F. 1247), (J. 24), (+III.)

This species, which is a cold-weather visitor to India, is very like No. 158 in habits and appearance. It is, however, characterised by having long legs. It is bolder and swifter in its movements. (Illus. B. D., p. 84; also B. B., p. 21.)

160. *Falco jugger:* The Laggar Falcon. (F. 1257), (J. 11), (+III.)

Several species of falcon occur in India. This one is, I think, the commonest.

It is a brownish bird barred and spotted all over with white. It looks like a large sparrow-hawk with long pointed wings. But it does not make one dash at its prey after the manner of the sparrow-hawk; it is a strong flier and settles down to a long chase in the open country. Its eyes are dark. Natives call falcons dark-eyed hawks, and sparrow-hawks light-eyed hawks.

161. *Æsalon chicquera:* The Turumti, or Red-headed Merlin. (F. 1264), (J. 16), (+III.)

Head and a stripe on the cheek chestnut. Back and tail grey barred with dark brown; under parts whitish with black streaks and bars.

This species lives largely on small birds and often hunts in couples.

162. *Tinnunculus alaudaris:* The Kestrel; the English "Windhover." (F. 1265), (J. 17), (+III.)

Head, neck, and tail grey, back and wings brick-red. Lower parts cream-coloured spotted with brown. The red back makes the bird easy to identify, as does its method of hunting its quarry. It flies over the open country, and every now and then hovers on rapidly vibrating wings over some spot where it thinks it espies some lizard or other animal. If there is an animal there it drops quietly on it, otherwise it passes on and hovers elsewhere.

It is a winter visitor to the plains of India.

The Green Pigeons, 163–164

These beautiful birds are strictly arboreal. They go about in small companies, but so closely do they assimilate in colour to their leafy surroundings that it is difficult to make them out. They feed exclusively on fruit.

163. *Crocopus phœnicopterus:* The Bengal Green Pigeon. (F. 1271), (J. 772), (+III.)

A bright yellowish-green bird. Head, lower breast, and tail dove colour. Some lilac and a yellow bar on the wing. Legs orange-yellow.

Found in the Eastern Punjab, U. P., and Bengal. In the Punjab, U. P., and the whole of the peninsula of India is found the next species.

164. *Crocopus chlorogaster:* The Southern Green Pigeon. (F. 1272), (J. 773), (+II.)

This is so like No. 163 that it seems scarcely deserving of specific rank. It differs only in having the lower breast green instead of grey.

165. *Columba intermedia:* The Indian Blue Rock Pigeon. (F. 1292), (J. 788), (+III.)

This familiar bird scarcely needs description. It is the common *Kabutar*. It is a bluish-grey bird (light slate colour) with two broad black bars across the wing. The tip of the tail is black; legs red.

Found all over India. In the Punjab this species meets an allied form—*Columba livia*—which is distinguished by the fact that its lower back is white instead of slaty grey.

The Doves, 166–169

Every one is well acquainted with these familiar birds, so that a general description of them is unnecessary. The four species most commonly seen in India are:

166. *Turtur suratensis:* The Spotted Dove. (F. 1307), (J. 795), (III.)

A reddish-grey bird. The sides of the neck are black with a number of small white spots. The two median pairs of tail feathers are brown, and the others black with white tips.

Its note is a plaintive *cŭkoo-coo-coo.* Like the other three species of dove this species is widely distributed, but is very capricious in its distribution.

It is very common in Calcutta, Madras, Travancore, Tirhoot, and Lucknow, but does not occur at Lahore, Bombay, or in the Deccan.

It is easily distinguished from the other doves by its black tippet. (Illus. F. IV., p. 1; also B. C., p. 123, and B. D., p. 8.)

167. *Turtur cambayensis:* The Little Brown Dove. (F. 1309), (J. 794), (– III; midway between the bulbul and myna in size.)

This pretty little dove often nests in the verandah, building on the rolled-up *chiks.*

Eha thus describes it: "Of an earthy brown colour, passing into slaty grey on the wings and tail, and tinged on the head, neck, and breast with that tender tint peculiar to doves, which the natural history books call 'vinaceous,' like a faded claret stain on the tablecloth. On each side of the neck there is a miniature chess-board in red and black. The feet are red." Its call is composed of quite a little tune—a soft, subdued, musical *cuk-cuk-coo-coo-coo.*

This dove is capriciously distributed. It is common in the Punjab, U. P., Deccan, Bombay, but absent in Lower Bengal and the Malabar coast.

168. *Turtur risorius:* The Indian Ring Dove. (F. 1310), (J. 796), (+III.)

This bird is a light French grey. It is distinguishable from Nos. 166 and 167 by its paler hue and by the possession of a black collar with a narrow white border round the back of the neck. Its note is a *ku-ku—kū.*

It is common in the Punjab, U. P., and the Deccan. It is found in Assam and S. India on the East, but not on the West Coast, nor in Lower Bengal.

169. *Œnopopelia tranquebarica:* The Red Turtle Dove. (F. 1311), (J. 797), (II.)

This is the smallest of the doves, and is not nearly so abundant as the other three species. In the U. P. it is a permanent resident, but in the Punjab merely a summer emigrant. It certainly is not common in most parts of South India. It is remarkable in that the cock and hen differ in appearance.

The cock is a grey bird with a black collar round the back of his neck, and reddish wings.

The hen lacks the red on the wing.

The note is harsh and sepulchral, more like a grunt than a *coo.* The legs are not red as in the other common doves.

The Sand Grouse

This family seems to form a connecting link between the pigeons and the gallinaceous birds. They are characterised by having feathered legs. They are coloured so as to assimilate closely to their sandy surroundings. They are game birds. The reader is therefore referred to Marshall and Hume's standard book, in which there are coloured plates of the various species. The order is treated of on pp. 53–63 of Vol. IV. of the Bird Volumes of *The Fauna of British India* series. (Illus. I. G. I., pp. 43, 47, 53, 57, 59, 65, 69, 77.)

170. *Pavo cristatus:* The Common Peafowl. (F. 1324), (J. 803), (+V, with a long train in the cock.)

Description of this familiar bird is unnecessary, but it and its loud call, like the *miau* of a cat, are known to all men.

The Quails

These, being game birds, do not come within the scope of the present work. The reader is referred to Hume and Marshall and the Bird Volumes of *The Fauna of British India* series for accounts of them. Since, however, one sometimes, in the course of a walk in the cold weather, puts up a common quail, I will briefly describe the bird. As you walk along you suddenly hear a rustling noise almost at your feet, and before you can say "Jack Robinson" a small brown bird has arisen with a flutter and dashed off a few inches over the tops of the heads of corn in the adjacent field. After a flight of twenty or thirty yards the bird drops into the corn—that is all you are likely to see of the quail unless you shoot it or net it.

171. *Coturnix communis:* The Common or Grey Quail. (F. 1355), (J. 829), (+II, but with a very short tail.)

A brown bird much spotted and barred with black, having some white streaks along the length of the back. Short legs.

A winter visitor to India. (Illus. I. G. II., p. 133.)

The Partridges

These are game birds, and so lie outside the scope of this book. I will, however, describe briefly two common species, whose calls are to be numbered among the commonest sounds heard in the jungle.

172. *Francolinus vulgaris:* The Black Partridge, or Common Francolin. (F. 1372), (J. 818), (+III.)

The cock is a handsome black bird, with

everywhere narrow bars of white or grey. The sides of the head are white, and there is a broad chestnut collar all round the neck.

The hen is reddish brown in most places where the cock is black.

Its cry is a curious harsh crow, so high-pitched as to be inaudible to some human beings. Indian Muhammedans declare that the bird calls "*Sub-hān, teri kudrat.*" Blanford syllabises it as, "*Juk-juk, tee-tee-tur.*"

It is found in N. India, most abundantly in the U. P. (Illus. I. G. II., p. 9.)

173. *Francolinus pondicerianus:* The Grey Partridge. (F. 1375), (J. 822), (+III.)

A greyish-brown bird marked all over with thin white or buff cross bars.

The loud call of this bird must be familiar to most Anglo-Indians. It is uttered early in the morning and again at sunset. Blanford describes it as "beginning with two or three single harsh notes, and continuing with a succession of trisyllabic, shrill, ringing cries." Jerdon says of this species: "Its call is a peculiar loud shrill cry, and has, not unaptly, been compared to the word *Pateela-pateela-pateela*, quickly repeated, but preceded by a single note uttered two or three times, each time with a higher intonation, till it gets, as it were, the key-note of its call."

This species runs very fast, and does not, as a rule, take to its wings unless flushed. (I. G. II. p. 51, but plate not a good one.)

The Rails, 174–176

174. *Amaurornis phœnicurus:* The White-breasted Water-hen. (F. 1401), (J. 907), (+II.)

A dark slaty-grey bird, almost black, with a white face, throat, and breast. The under parts of the tail, which is carried almost erect, are chestnut red. Wherever there is a pond having near it some bamboos or rushes there is one likely to see a water-hen. It is a great skulker, and always makes for cover the moment it thinks it is being watched. "It is," as Blanford remarks, "an excessively noisy bird; its loud, hoarse, reiterated call, predominating in the evening and morning over the cries of the other waders and the ducks in the village tank, must be familiar to most people in India." (Illus. B. B., p. 173.)

175. *Porphyrio poliocephalus:* The Purple Moorhen, or Purple Coot. (F. 1404), (J. 902), (IV.)

A beautiful purple-blue bird with very long red legs. The bill is red, as is a square shield which the bird carries on its forehead. It has a white patch under its tail. It is impossible to mistake this bird. There is none other like unto it in India. One frequently comes across it when out shooting.

176. ***Fulica atra*:** The Coot. (F. 1405), (J. 903), (IV.)

This is the most duck-like of all the rails, and indeed is very frequently shot and eaten as a duck by inexperienced sportsmen. However, its shining black plumage and its white bill and shield on the forehead serve to differentiate it from all Indian ducks. Moreover, when disturbed on the water, it experiences some difficulty in starting to fly. It runs along the surface of the water for a few feet with vigorous flappings of the wings and much splashing before it succeeds in lifting itself out of the water. It does not usually keep in flocks as ducks do. It breeds in India. It does not swim so high in the water as a duck. Its feet are not webbed, but its toes are pinnate, i.e. provided with flattened membranes which assist it in swimming. Its bill is not so flat as that of a duck.

The Cranes, 177–179

Cranes are large, tall, long-shanked birds which have a loud, trumpet-like call. The three common Indian species are chiefly grey in colour. They never perch in trees, but rest and nest on the ground. When they fly they carry the neck and feet stretched out straight. When they fly in company the flight takes a V-shaped form, like that of a flight of geese.

177. *Grus communis:* The Common Crane. (F. 1407), (J. 865), (+V; about twice the size of a kite.)

This bird is the *coolung* of sportsmen. Its general colour is dark French grey. Its head is almost devoid of feathers, and there is a square, dark red patch of skin across the back of the head. It has a broad white band running down each side of the long neck. Its legs are black.

It is a winter visitor to India. It is fairly common in N. India, but rare in the south.

It is usually seen in flocks, which spend the middle of the day on sandbanks in the middle of rivers. (Illus. I. G. III., p. 21.)

178. *Grus antigone:* The Sarus. (F. 1409),

(J. 863), (+V. This is the largest of the Indian cranes, and stands nearly as high as a human being.)

Its general hue is French grey. Its head is devoid of feathers. Its throat and a ring round the nape are black. Its head and neck are red. Its legs are dull red.

It is the most familiar of the Indian cranes. It is usually seen in pairs. It does not soar high in the air, like the other two species. It is a permanent resident, but does not appear to occur south of the Godaveri.

It is far more confidential than the other species of crane, and will sometimes allow a human being to approach within thirty yards of it. (Illus. I. G. III., p. 1, but plate is not good.)

179. *Anthropoides virgo:* The Demoiselle Crane. (F. 1411), (J. 866), (+V. The smallest of the cranes.)

This bird is sometimes wrongly called *coolung* by sportsmen; the Hindustani name for it is *Karkarra*.

A light grey bird, with a black face and neck and some black in the wings. Behind the eye is a streak of white feathers which ends in a long graceful white plume. Its note is harsher and less trumpet-like than those of the other cranes.

It is a winter visitor to India. It is very common in the Deccan, Guzerat, and Kattiwar; less common in other parts of N. India, and rare in Lower Bengal and S. India. Its habits are like those of No. 177. (Illus. F. IV., p. 184; also I. G. III., p. 31.)

The Bustards

These come within the category of "game birds," and so none of them are treated of in this book. (Illus. I. G. I., pp. 1, 3, 7, 18.)

180. *Œdicnemus scolopax:* The Stone-Curlew, or Stone-Plover, or Thick-knee. (F. 1418), (J. 859), (+IV.)

This bird is very like a bustard, and is known to Anglo-Indian sportsmen as the *Bustard-Florican.* It is an ashy-brown bird, each feather having a blackish streak down the shaft. Its wings and tail have some black and white bars, which are conspicuous when the bird flies. The bill, eyes, and feet are yellow. Its wild-sounding cry, which is often heard at night, is like that of the curlew.

It frequents dry, open, stony country.

The Jaçanas, 181 *and* 182

These remarkable birds have very long toes, which enable them to run about on the large floating leaves of water plants.

181. *Metopidius indicus:* The Bronze-winged Jaçana. (F. 1428), (J. 900), (– IV.)

Head, neck, and breast a beautiful glossy black. A conspicuous white eyebrow. There is some black in the wings, but the general hue of these is a metallic greenish bronze. The lower back and tail are chestnut red.

Rare in Western India; common in the east.

"They present," writes Cunningham, "an odd appearance on the wing, owing to the disproportionate size of their feet, which becomes particularly conspicuous when the legs are dropped just before the bird pitches on the surface of the weeds and expands its toes, which have been gathered up into a bundle during flight."

182. *Hydrophasianus chirurgus:* The Pheasant-tailed Jaçana. (F. 1429), (J. 901), (IV, but with a tail a foot in length in the breeding season.)

Winter plumage: Upper parts brown, with

a conspicuous white eyebrow and a yellow band down each side of the neck. Wings black and white. Lower parts white with a black gorget across the breast. Tail feathers white, except the two median ones, which are brown.

Breeding plumage: A long black pheasant-like tail is assumed, and the other parts are black, save the head, throat, and wings, which are white, and the back of the neck, which is golden yellow. This Jaçana looks in breeding plumage (i.e. in the summer) rather like a silver pheasant, and, indeed, Europeans call it the water-pheasant. It is a beautiful creature in its summer splendour. Finn says that it is to his mind "the most beautiful of all our smaller aquatic birds, and hardly equalled in this respect by any bird whatever."

Its peculiar wailing cry has been likened to the mew of a kitten.

The Lapwings, 183 *and* 184

183. *Sarcogrammus indicus:* The Red-wattled Lapwing. (F. 1431), (J. 855), (+IV.)

This is the familiar "Did-you-do-it."

Head, neck, and upper breast black. There

is a broad white band running from the eye down the whole length of the neck. The back and wings are bronzy brown, black, and white, the white being arranged so as to form a conspicuous bar during flight. Lower parts are white, as is the tail, except for a black band which runs across it near the tip. The bill is reddish, and there is in front of the eye a conspicuous crimson wattle. The legs are bright yellow.

This noisy bird is known to all residents in India. Its noisy call, " Did he do it ? Pity to do it," is one of the most familiar sounds of the Indian country-side. (Illus. B. B., p. 161.)

In Burma it is replaced by an allied species—*Sarcogrammus atrinuchalis*—the Burmese Wattled Lapwing.

184. *Saciophorus malabaricus:* The Yellow-wattled Lapwing. (F. 1433), (J. 856), (–IV.)

This is very like the last species, the chief difference being that the conspicuous wattle is yellow instead of crimson and the white line runs round the back of the head from eye to eye, instead of down the neck. Its cry is like that of No. 183, but not so harsh and with a note less.

This species is widely distributed, but not

usually so common as the last. It is said not to occur in Upper Sind or the Western Punjab. It certainly does not occur in the neighbourhood of Lahore.

The Plovers, 185 *and* 186

The ringed plovers are small "snippets" which haunt the seashore and the sandbanks of rivers. They go about in small flocks. Numbers of them are to be seen on the muddy edges of the Coum at Madras, but they have to be looked for, since from a little distance they assimilate closely to the hue of the mudbanks on which they disport themselves. They are not much bigger than sparrows, but are pretty little birds. Two species are common.

185. *Ægialitis alexandrina:* The Kentish Plover. (F. 1446), (J. 848), (I.)

Upper parts brown, lower parts white. The brown of the upper parts is broken by a white forehead, eyebrow, and collar. The under surface of the wing is white, so that as a flock of this species or the next two species fly they look now brown, now white, according as the brown or white surface of the wing is presented to the observer.

This species is seen chiefly in winter and on the sea-coast.

186. *Ægialitis dubia:* The Little Ringed Plover. (F. 1447), (J. 850), (I.)

This is very like No. 185 in appearance, but may be easily distinguished from it by having a black band across the throat. Legs yellow.

This species is not confined to the sea-coast. Like most of its tribe it has a plaintive whistle.

187. *Himantopus candidus:* The Black-winged Stilt, or Long-legs. (F. 1451), (J. 898), (– IV.)

Male: A white bird with glossy black back and wings.

Female: White with brown back and wings.

This species is characterised by very long red legs. Its bill is nearly three inches long.

It is found in marshes and tanks.

188. *Recurvirostra avocetta:* The Avocet. (F. 1452), (J. 899), (IV.)

This elegant bird is characterised by a very long bill, which is curved *upwards* towards the end. It is a very easy bird to identify. Its body is about the size of that of the crow. It is a white bird with a number of black markings. The black markings are on top of the head, back of the neck, the shoulders, and the wings. The beak is black and the long legs are dark grey.

Wherever there is shallow water there may the avocet be found wading in winter, for it is only a winter visitor to India. It does not appear to be very common anywhere.

The Curlews, 189 *and* 190

189. *Numenius arquata:* The Curlew. (F. 1454), (J. 877), (V.)

This well-known bird is about the size of a kite, and except for the white chin and throat its colouring is rather like that of the kite. But here all resemblance to the kite ceases. The curlew is a long-shanked wading bird, with a curved bill half a foot in length, the curve in this case being downwards instead of upwards as in the avocet. It has a wild, plaintive cry.

It is a winter visitor to India.

190. *Numenius phæopus:* The Whimbrel. (F. 1455), (J. 878), (+IV; about midway between the crow and the kite.)

This is a small edition of the curlew, but differs from it in having a white band along the middle of the head. Its curved bill is only a little over three inches long. It is less abundant than the curlew, and perhaps scarcely deserves a place among the common birds of India.

191. *Limosa belgica:* The Black-tailed Godwit. (F. 1456), (J. 875), (– V.)

A brown bird with white chin, throat, and abdomen, and some white in the wings. The base of the tail is white and the remainder black. The bill is about four inches long, and straight. The legs are long.

A winter visitor to India; common in the north and rare in the south.

Blanford states that it is often sold in the Calcutta bazaar as woodcock, but Finn states that this is not in accordance with his experience. (Illus. I. G. III., p. 409.)

The Sandpipers, 192–195

These birds constitute the "snippets" of Anglo-Indian, that is to say, birds that try to be snipe.

These are all greenish-brown birds with light under parts. They have fairly long bills, but not so long as that of any of the species of snipe. They are often seen feeding—a statement which cannot be made regarding the snipe. If you see a snipe-like bird feeding, you may be perfectly sure that it is not a snipe. It is a sandpiper of sorts, but it is not by any means easy to say which of the many sandpipers without shooting it. Descriptions of the common species of sandpiper follow :—

192. *Totanus hypoleucus :* The Common Sandpiper. (F. 1460), (J. 893), (+II, but with a very short tail, so that it actually measures less than a bulbul.)

It is a greenish-brown bird with white under parts. Its legs are not long for a wader ; its bill is about an inch long. It goes about in ones or twos (never in flocks), picking up insects on the water's edge. When disturbed it flies away, and then its wings, which are pointed, show a very narrow white band. By this you may recognise the species. It flies low, and as Eha remarks, with its wings bent like a bow. When it settles down it wags its apology for a tail in wagtail-like manner. (Illus. B. B., p. 168.)

193. *Totanus glareola :* The Wood Sandpiper, or Spotted Sandpiper. (F. 1461), (J. 891), (+II, but with a very short tail.)

The upper plumage of this is dark brown

spotted with white. The abdomen is white, as is also the tail.

The habits of this species are very like those of the snipe, so that the sportsman out shooting constantly puts up the bird, but it can be distinguished from the snipe, because instead of emitting the sharp "*psip*" of the snipe on rising, it utters a shrill note. Moreover, it is a much smaller bird than even the Jack-snipe.

194. *Totanus ochropus:* The Green Sandpiper. (F. 1462), (J. 892), (+II, but with a short tail.)

This bird is very like the last species, except that it is larger and less conspicuously spotted, and has more white in the tail. It is distinguishable from the snipe, alongside of which it is often found, by its "shrill piping note," which it utters on the wing, and its white tail, which is conspicuous as it flies away.

A winter visitor; commoner in N. India than in the south.

195. *Tringa minuta:* The Little Stint. (F. 1471), (J. 884), (+I, but with a short tail.)

Upper parts dingy brown, with white forehead and under parts.

"If," writes Eha, "you see a hundred dingy little birds, about the size of sparrows, all feeding together knee-deep in water, you may safely put them down as stints."

A winter visitor to India ; common on the coasts.

The Snipes

These being game birds are not dealt with in this volume. It must suffice that all four species—The Common, Full, or Fantail Snipe (*Gallinago cœlestis*), The Pintail (*G. stenura*), The Little Jack-Snipe (*G. gallinula*), and The Painted Snipe (*Rostratula capensis*), who is not a true snipe, all lie up closely in marshy ground or paddy fields in the daytime, and are not likely to be seen by the naturalist unless he is prepared to wade and flush them.

When flushed the first three go off at a great pace, either uttering no call or a short, sharp "*psip*." The flight of the last species is comparatively feeble. (Illus. I. G. III., pp. 339, 359, etc.)

The Gulls, 196–199

Gulls are very familiar birds to every one who has performed the journey from England to India. The beautiful flight and the loud screams of these kites of the sea are indelibly impressed upon the memory of most Anglo-Indians.

These magnificent fliers are able to keep pace with the steamer for hours at a time without putting forth any effort. They saunter through the air in the wake of the ship, and when anything edible is thrown overboard they drop down and pick it off the water (they can swim like ducks), and having devoured what there is to be eaten, they fly on after the ship, and catch it up in a few seconds.

They are largely scavengers. At sea-coast stations no sight is more familiar than that of a number of crows and gulls squabbling over the little fish, etc., that the fishermen throw away when overhauling their nets on the sea-shore. (Illus. B. D., p. 272; also B. B., p. 190.)

The three commonest gulls in India are:

196. *Larus ridibundus*: The Laughing Gull. (F. 1490), (J. 981), (IV.)

A white bird with grey shoulders and some black in the wings. In summer the head and neck become brown and in winter traces of this usually remain. The bill and legs are red.

A winter visitor to India.

197. *Larus brunneicephalus:* The Brown-headed Gull. (F. 1491), (J. 980), (+IV.)

This bird is very like the last at all seasons, so that it is scarcely possible to distinguish them on the wing.

198. *Larus affinis:* The Dark-backed Herring-Gull. (F. 1494), (J. 978), (V.)

This bird is distinguished from Nos. 196 and 197 by the fact that its wings and shoulders are slate-grey instead of pale grey, and its legs are yellow. It is a much larger bird than the above two species.

It is said to be very common at Karachi. It is found on other parts of the West Coast, but apparently not on the East Coast.

199. *Larus cachinans:* The Yellow-legged Herring-Gull. (F. 1495), (V.)

This is very like No. 198, except that its shoulders are of a lighter shade of grey. It has yellow legs.

This gull is often seen on the rivers and large *jhils* of Northern India in winter.

The Terns, 200–205

These beautiful birds have been aptly termed the swallows of the sea, for like swallows they are birds of powerful flight, and remain for long periods on the wing. But they are not confined to the sea. In India, wherever there are rivers, *jhils*, or ponds there are terns to be found.

Their prevailing colour is white, and most of them have some black in their plumage.

To repeat what I said in *Bombay Ducks:* "No one can fail to recognise a tern. If you see a slenderly-built bird of whitish tinge, with long swallow-like wings and forked tail, a bird which sails along easily over water, sometimes diving for a fish, more frequently picking something off the surface of the water, you may set that bird down as a tern." (Illus. B. D., p. 270.)

200. *Hydrochelidon hybrida:* The Whiskered Tern, or the Small Marsh Tern. (F. 1496), (J. 984), (+II.)

Winter plumage: A white bird with grey back, wings, and tail. Some black on the nape of the neck and a black streak behind the eye. Bill, legs, and toes dull red.

Summer plumage: The whole of the upper part of the head is black.

Very common in N. India. An inland bird found on marshes, rivers, tanks, and paddy fields.

201. *Hydroprogne caspia:* The Caspian Tern. (F. 1498), (J. 982), (+IV.)

This is the largest of the terns. It is a white bird save for the fact that there is a good deal of black in the head. Its wings are pearl grey. Its bill is bright red. Its legs are black. Its tail is not very deeply forked. It goes about in pairs. It is local in its distribution.

It is common at Madras, and is said to be párticularly common in Sind. I have never seen it in the Punjab. Eha does not mention it as one of the birds of Bombay.

202. *Sterna angelica:* The Gull-billed Tern. (F. 1499), (J. 983), (+III, with a longish tail.)

Printer's devils are particularly spiteful to this bird. In *The Common Birds of Bombay* they have mutilated its name into "gull-gilled." In *Bombay Ducks* it appears as the "gull-bird tern."

It is the least beautiful of the terns, being more heavily built than most of them.

In winter it is a white bird with grey wings and some black in the head. In summer its head is jet black. The bill, legs, and feet are black. Its tail is not very deeply forked.

It is found both inland and on the coast.

203. *Sterna seena:* The Indian River Tern.

(F. 1503), (J. 985), (+III, with a long, deeply forked tail.)

This is the common tern of N. India, and frequents all the large rivers.

Its head and nape are deep black. The upper plumage French grey. Lower plumage very pale grey. Chin white, and a white patch on each cheek. Bill bright deep yellow. Legs red. This bird moults about Christmas time, and for a few weeks after the moult there is much white in the head, but this soon disappears.

204. *Sterna melanogaster :* The Black-bellied Tern. (F. 1504), (J. 987), (–III, but with a long, deeply forked tail.)

Head black (with some white after the moult at Christmas), *abdomen black*. Cheek, chin, throat, and wing lining white. Rest of plumage grey, paler on the tail than on the back. Bill orange-yellow; legs and feet dull red.

One of the commonest of the terns, especially inland.

205. *Sterna minuta :* The Little Tern. (F. 1510), (J. 988), (–II.)

A tern not much bigger than a sparrow, with a white forehead and black head, white cheeks and lower parts, grey wings, dark red bill and legs, is probably this species.

It is fairly common in N. India ; rare in the south.

206. *Rhynchops albicollis :* The Indian Skimmer, or Scissors-bill. (F. 1517), (J. 995), (–IV.)

A long-winged, tern-like bird, which flies about in little flocks a few inches above the surface of the water, with white forehead, tail, and lower parts, and a white collar round the neck ; rest of upper plumage dark brown. Bill deep red ; legs bright red. (Illus. F. IV., p. 296.)

The Pelicans, 207 *and* 208

Description of these well-known birds is superfluous, as every one knows what they look like.

Four species are found in India, but they can scarcely be described as common birds. Two species, however, are fairly abundant on the big *jhils* of Northern India.

207. *Pelicanus crispus :* The Dalmatian Pelican. (F. 1522), (+V ; a large bird as big as a swan.)

The beak is one and a half feet in length. A white bird with some black in the wings. Bill dark grey.

Winter visitor to U. P. and Sind. (Illus. F. IV., p. 331.)

208. *Pelicanus philippensis:* The Spotted-billed or Grey Pelican. (F. 1523), (J. 1004), (+V; much smaller than 207.)

This may be distinguished by the curious dark spots and markings on its pinkish-yellow bill. (Illus. B. P., frontispiece.)

The Cormorants, 209–211

These are large black birds, which live largely on the water, and catch fish by diving. When not fishing they have the habit of standing on top of a post with wings outspread and then look rather like a church lectern.

Three species occur in India:

209. *Phalacrocorax carbo:* The Large Cormorant. (F. 1526), (J. 1005), (+V.)

210. *Phalacrocorax fuscicollis:* The Indian Shag. (F. 1527), (J. 1006), (+V, but smaller than 209.)

211. *Phalacrocorax javanicus:* The Little Cormorant. (F. 1528), (J. 1007), (IV.)

All three have similar habits, the last being the only common member of the genus. No. 210 has no white throat. Nos. 209 and 211 have a white throat, but can be readily distinguished by the fact that No. 209 is one foot longer than No. 211.

The Ibises, 212–214

Ibises are birds about the size of a common fowl, but having a long curved bill like that of the curlew. As Finn has pointed out, "Ibises fly like storks with the neck outstretched, but with a quicker stroke of the wings and frequent intervals of sailing with the pinions held level, so that they are easily distinguished from other waders when on the wing." They usually occur in small flocks.

212. *Ibis melanocephala:* The White Ibis. (F. 1541), (J. 941), (+V.)

The bald head and neck are black, as are the long bill and legs. The rest of the plumage is white.

213. *Inocotis papillosus:* The Black Ibis. (F. 1542), (J. 942), (+V.)

The Black Curlew, or King Curlew, or King Ibis of Anglo-Indians.

In this species the head only, and not the neck as in No. 212, is devoid of feathers. The skin is black, but the back of the head is covered with little red warts. The plumage is glossy black, save for a small white patch on the wing. The bill, which is nearly six inches long, is dull dark green. Legs bright red.

214. *Plegadis falcinellus:* The Glossy Ibis. (F. 1544), (J. 943), (+V.)

In this species only the front of the face is devoid of feathers. A chestnut bird with head, wings, and tail dark brown with a green gloss.

215. *Platalea leucorodia:* The Spoonbill. (F. 1545), (J. 939), (+V.)

A large white bird with a crest in the breeding season. The long bill, which is flat and expanded at the end like a spoon, is black, as are the long legs. It is impossible to mistake spoonbills. There are no other birds like them. They are found in small flocks on sandbanks, etc., at the water's edge.

The Storks, 216–221

Every one is familiar with the appearance of the common stork. The leading features of the stork family are their large size, their long legs, neck, and bill, and their perching habits. In this last respect they differ from cranes, which never perch in trees. During flight their long necks are stretched out forwards, and their long legs stretched out backwards. They fly by a slow, steady flapping of the wings, but often sail on outstretched wings like vultures. Their nests are in India, huge platforms of sticks built in trees.

216. *Ciconia alba*: The White Stork. (F. 1546), (J. 919), (+V; 3½ feet long.)

A white bird with some black in the wings. Bill and legs bright red.

A winter visitor, common in North India.

217. *Dissura episcopus*: The White-necked Stork, or the Beefsteak Bird. (F. 1548), (J. 920), (+V; 3 feet long.)

A black bird, except for the neck and lower parts, which are white. Bill black; legs dull red.

Not found in Punjab or Sind.

218. *Xenorhynchus asiaticus*: The Black-necked Stork. Sportsmen call this bird the Australian Stork. (F. 1549), (J. 917), (+V; 4½ feet long.)

Beak, head, neck, and shoulders black; wings black and white. Rest of plumage white; legs bright red.

219. *Leptoptilus dubius:* The Adjutant. (F. 1550), (J. 915), (+V; 5 feet long.)

This huge bird is characterised by an enormous beak, over a foot in length, and a head devoid of feathers. From its neck hangs a pouch. There is a ruff of white feathers round the neck. The lower parts are white. The wings are partly dark slaty grey and partly French grey. The bill is dirty pink, and the legs dirty greyish white.

Not found in S. India. (Illus. B. P., pp. 28 and 34; also I. F., p. 232.)

220. *Pseudotantalus leucocephalus:* The Painted Stork. The Pelican Ibis of old writers. (F. 1552), (J. 938), (+V; 3½ feet long.)

This is a stork which is trying to turn into an ibis; its bill, which is ten inches long, having a marked downward curve. It is a white bird with a black band across the breast. The wings are mainly black.

The front of the head is devoid of feathers and is orange-yellow, as is the bill. The legs are brown.

Not found in the Punjab; very common in the Deccan. (Its head is figured in Vol. IV., p. 376 of O. and B. B.)

221. *Anastomus oscitans:* The Open-Bill. The Shell Ibis of the older writers. (F. 1553), (J. 940), (+V; nearly 3 feet long.)

This bird is distingushed from all others by the fact that the mandibles do not meet in the middle; indeed the beak looks as though it had become distorted owing to the attempts of the bird to crack a very hard nut! (The head is figured on p. 378, F. IV.) It is a greyish-white bird with black shoulders, wings, and tail. The bill is light horn colour, and the legs dirty pink.

To my mind this bird looks like a white stork that sadly needs a wash and brush up and its beak put straight!

Found only in N. India. Abundant in Oudh and Bengal.

The Herons, 222–225

Herons are wading birds with long, sharp, stiletto-like bills and telescopic necks. It is their habit to stand motionless in shallow water with the head almost buried on the shoulders. When a victim shows itself, out shoots the neck of the fisher, and woe betide his victim! On the wing herons are easily identified by their large size, the steady flapping of their wings, and the fact that they fly with the neck drawn in and the legs projecting behind beyond the tail. A great many species of heron occur in India, but only four are commonly seen by the average observer.

222. *Ardea cinerea:* The Common Heron. This is the familiar heron of England. (F. 1555), (J. 923), (+V; a little over a yard long.)

An ashy-grey bird with some white on the head. From the back of the head some black plumes hang. Lower parts white. Bill dark yellow. Legs dirty green.

Usually a solitary bird.

223. *Bubulcus coromandus:* The Cattle Egret. (F. 1562), (J. 929), (+IV.)

A pure white bird with a yellow bill and black legs. In the breeding season some yellow plumes grow from the back of the head.

This is a sociable species. These birds frequently accompany cattle, which serve as efficient beaters. The quadrupeds put up grasshoppers, etc., which the egrets seize. The birds sometimes perch on the backs of cattle.

There are three larger species of egret which are also white; these belong to the genus *Herodias*, but these are scarcely common birds.

A large white egret with the bill black is one of these species. (Illus. B. D., p. 240.)

224. *Ardeola grayi:* The Pond Heron. This is the ubiquitous Paddy Bird. (F. 1565), (J. 930), (+IV.)

This bird, which may be seen squatting at the margin of every tank and every village pond, looks greenish brown—much the colour of its muddy surroundings. But startle it and it opens out milk-white wings on which it flies away with steady flappings. It is impossible to mistake a paddy bird. It sits all brown and flies all white. Close inspection shows that every feather has the shaft of a colour different from the web. (Illus. B. D., p. 236; also B. P., p. 114; also B. B., p. 178.)

225. *Nycticorax griseus:* The Night Heron. (F. 1568), (J. 937), (V.)

A large dusky-coloured bird which is seen flapping its way along about sunset with loud raucous cries that sound like "*wāk*" is the night heron.

The head, nape, back, and shoulders are black. Forehead, cheek, breast, and lower parts white. Remainder of plumage ashy grey. Eyes bright red. Some of the feathers of the back of the neck are white and are lengthened to form plumes. (Illus. B. D., pp. 232 and 238.)

226. *Phœnicopterus roseus:* The Common Flamingo. (F. 1575), (J. 944), (+V; nearly 4½ feet long.)

These beautiful birds occur in flocks in shallow lakes. They are white with a pink tinge. The wings are white, black, and cerise. The long legs are deep pink. The curious beak is bent in the middle to form an obtuse angle. (The beak is figured on p. 408 of Vol. IV. of O. and B. B.)

The Geese, 227 *and* 228

As geese are game birds they do not come strictly within the scope of this book. However, as these birds are much *en evidence* in Upper India in the cold weather, I will briefly describe the two common species.

In the U. P. during the winter months no sight is more common than that of a V-shaped flock of geese cleaving its way through the air on quivering wings. The birds, as they fly, utter a curious cackle easy to recognise, but difficult to describe. This call is often heard at night. When riding in the early morning one often surprises a flock of geese feeding in some field. They pass the day on a sandbank in some large river, most of the flock asleep on one leg with heads tucked under the wing, but one or two birds are invariably posted as sentinels.

227. *Anser ferus:* The Grey-lag Goose. (F. 1579), (J. 945), (V.)

Upper parts brown, the shoulders having a number of narrow pale cross bars. Lower parts pale grey. Bill, legs, and feet are a dirty pink colour.

Not found in S. India. (Illus. I. G. III., p. 55.)

228. *Anser indicus:* The Barred-headed Goose. (F. 1583), (J. 949), (–V.)

This species is distinguished from the other by its yellow bill and feet, and the fact that its head is white with two conspicuous broad black cross bars, from which the bird derives its name. Its general colour is more grey than that of the last species.

Rare in S. India. (Illus. I. D., p. 84; also I. G. III., p. 81.)

The Ducks, 229 and 230

These being game birds do not come within the scope of this work. Two species, however, which are commonly seen are not usually shot by sportsmen on account of their indifferent flavour. These I describe.

229. *Casarca rutila:* The Ruddy Sheldrake, or Brahminy Duck. (F. 1588), (J. 954), (– V.)

This is a curious pale ruddy-brown bird, whitish on the head. Tail and wings black. Bill, legs, and feet blackish.

This handsome duck is a winter visitor to India. It is very abundant in N. India, less abundant in S. India, not being found at all on the Malabar coast. It invariably goes about in pairs, which dwell in rivers rather than in tanks. They are wary birds and a great nuisance to sportsmen, since they warn other water-fowl of danger. "It is difficult," writes Blanford, "so long as one is on an Indian river to get out of sight of these birds or out of hearing of their peculiar clanging bi-syllabic call or alarm cry, which is uttered frequently on the smallest excuse." The cry is like a soft "*chakwa*," hence the Hindustani name of the bird. (Illus. I. D., p. 114; also I. G. III., p. 123.)

230. *Spatula clypeata*: The Shoveller. (F. 1602), (J. 957), (−V.)

This handsome duck, although it occurs in *jhils*, is pre-eminently a village duck. If there be any considerable piece of stagnant water near a village in N. India, there are likely to be some shoveller ducks on this—in winter, for they are only winter visitors to India. This species is distinguishable from other ducks by its great flat bill being much broader at the tip than at the base. It has a peculiar habit of swimming in circles with its bill resting on the surface of the water.

Cock, after February: Head and upper neck glossy green. Lower neck and breast white. Abdomen chestnut. Rest of body brown with a green patch or speculum in the wing.

Cock before February, and Hen: Reddish brown with a lighter-coloured border to many of the feathers. (Illus. I. D., p. 196; also I. G. III., p. 141.)

231. *Podicipes albipennis*: The Indian Little Grebe, or Dabchick. (F. 1617), (J. 975), (+II.)

This is one of the most aquatic birds in existence. It rarely walks on *terra firma*, and never takes to flight from the water. When alarmed it seeks safety by diving. Writing of this bird, Eha says, "I do not know how to describe it better than to say that you might take it for a small chicken without a tail. Its colour is dark glossy brown on the upper parts, with some rich chestnut on the sides of the neck. Young birds are lighter." (Illus. B. B., p. 184.)

THE END